DEN THERE WERE MORE

HIDDEN PACK SANCTUARY

MAGGIE DECKER

To all the fans that asked for more.

And to Nathan Fillion, no particular reason, I just really love him.

For the strength of the pack is the wolf, and the strength of the wolf is the pack.
   -Rudyard Kipling

Mariam was happy to see that Mark had stopped by, but concerned for the reason, nonetheless. The trip from Vegas was not a short one. She was still staying with her new in-laws in Oregon for at least a few more days and it made it a little more difficult to be Alpha when she was away from home. Eventually she was going to have to insist that Ben and Adam help her decide where they should live. There just hadn't been time since they met, it had been a whirlwind. A good thing, but a whirlwind, nonetheless.

"To what do I owe the pleasure?" Mariam asked while filling two plain green mugs with coffee. She carefully set them down on the breakfast counter, taking the barstool next to the one Mark was already seated on. "Don't get me wrong I'm ecstatic to see you, and very grateful that you're here to check on the pups, but I'm sure there is another reason you came all this way."

Mark smiled sadly at her before taking a restorative breath and answering. "I want to help. Sam is doing so much to find a cure and I need to help. I have some vacation time and I was hoping to use it to hang out and assist with trying to find a cure." Mariam tried to understand why he would've felt strongly enough about this that he'd come all the way to Oregon and obviously her curiosity was broadcast all over her face because Mark continued. "I'm so tired of treating the broken girls and beat up boys that have come in hurt because of people stronger than them who have apparently been infected with this damn virus. Or at least I'm hoping that most of them have the virus as an excuse." He looked lost for a minute and Mariam waited quietly, sipping her coffee, assuming correctly that he wasn't done speaking. "I don't know how I feel about the fact that the people I've been thinking of as 'bad guys' might not be truly at fault. I don't know if I can wrap my head around that. I think I may never forgive them and I'm not ready to feel that way about myself. Let me help, let me do something good while I still have some compassion left." Mark's voice was thick with unshed tears.

Mariam carefully sat down her mug and, looking up, took Mark's face in her hands. She gave him a gentle kiss on the forehead and spoke. "You are a saint among men but a man nonetheless, and you need to forgive yourself for the inability to forgive others. Other than the victims themselves you are the only other person that is so closely hurt by the foul deeds and exploits we are rescuing these people from. That being said, I think the people that are supposed to be working on this cure already are. I think you might be more useful elsewhere. Let me think about it and get back to you. Is that alright?"

"You're not just saying that are you? You will really let me help?"

His voice sounded far away and innocent.

Mariam reached out again, lightly squeezing the back of his neck. "Have I ever lied to you Mark? I love you like a brother and I'm your Alpha, I would not tell you I had a plan or idea if I didn't."

Mark nodded his head and sunk into the hand on the back of his neck. Mariam could feel how much he needed a strong alpha touch. "I know that, truly, I'm just feeling a bit off. I'm not sure what's wrong but I feel like something is coming."

Mariam believed him; she had no reason not to. "Then we will all be on alert, and careful. But for right now let me take you upstairs where my boys fell asleep feeding my girls."

~

*M*ark looked over both of the pups and proclaimed them healthy and adorable. Mariam tucked them back into their little bassinet and followed Mark back down to the kitchen. "They are absolutely the cutest little pups I've ever seen." Mariam smiled up at him.

"I think you're full of it, but since I like your little lie, I will just smile and say thank you."

Mariam grabbed a couple bottles of water out of the fridge and led Mark out the back door. They stopped at a gorgeous picnic table under a huge tree and took a seat.

Mariam took a swig from her water bottle and let out

a sigh. "So, your old Alpha has had a very drastic change to his pack."

Mark nodded. "So, I hear."

"I need a doctor out there at the campground, as soon as possible."

Mark didn't follow at first. "I'm not a doctor. Nor do I ever want to see that pack again."

Mariam nodded. "I understand that. I know how much you've been hurt by that pack. I have someone in mind but it's going to take some convincing and I think it might even take Joey's help to convince them."

Mark nodded. "She doesn't like pack. No, that's not right, she absolutely hates pack."

Mariam chuckled. "True. I'm going to have to beg." She reached a hand over and laid it on Mark's. "Am I going to have to beg you?"

Mark sighed and hung his head. "No. You don't have to beg; the guilt trip will suffice." They both laughed. "I wouldn't do this for anyone else, you know that right? And I can only give you my vacation days, so you better hurry and get her over there."

"I know." She gave his hand another little squeeze "I appreciate you more than you can ever know. You've saved my life so many times and now you're saving the pack. Even if the new members of our pack are people who did you wrong. That is big. Huge. It says more about you than you realize."

$\mathcal{M}$ark was still sitting at the gorgeous picnic table beneath the huge tree when he saw Joey and Elkan exit the workshop. He knew he needed to talk to Joey before he left, and even though he knew it was important, he was reluctant to interrupt what was obviously a sweet moment between the mates.

Catching Joey's eye, he headed over to them, meeting them halfway.

"What's up?" Joey's face was spread with a smile that was the obvious result of the sex that they both reeked of.

"Quick question, did Alpha tell you about the new additions to our pack and their need for a medical professional?" Mark inquired.

Joey's eyes opened wide, and he raised his eyebrows. "She did, but she didn't word it that way. Now that you did, I know exactly who you are going to recommend. I'll call her today or tomorrow; see how she feels about the prospect.

Mark smiled. "Thank you. I am heading out there to

be their temporary medic, but I can't stay. I just can't." With a final hug the two separated. He watched as Joey and Elkan headed out toward Elkan's SUV.

Mark headed back into the house to return the mug he'd brought out and say his farewells to everyone.

Mark loaded his luggage and himself back into his rental car along with the basket full of apple muffins and various snacks that Judy had made up for him. He loaded up the address of the campground the pack was at now, immediately noticing that it was in the middle of nowhere and guessing that he'd have zero phone service.

With that thought he sent a quick text message to Mariam that they were going to need to think about buying and installing a cell booster or two if they hadn't already.

~

Mark's drive had been longer than he liked but he was willing to do just about anything for the Alpha. She had saved him, body and soul and knew that she would do it all again. That kind of love and trust deserved loyalty in kind. Whenever he mentioned his feelings on the subject to her, she would shrug it off, claiming that he saved her first and they were even. He disagreed.

The road needed to be repaved. He was making a mental list of pack needs to give to Alpha. He was getting a little worried about his car because of the state of the road. He had to slow to a near crawl and it made the end of his already long 17-hour trip seem to take forever.

Finally, Mark saw the campground ahead, he pulled up

in front of the main lodge and parked next to a variety of other cars and rental trucks. His heart was beating out of his chest and so he took a few deep breaths to try to calm himself down.

It was different seeing them all last week. Last week he was amped up on adrenaline and righteous indignation. Plus, saving someone else and being a Good Samaritan always gave him nerves of steel. Alpha Mariam had been there too, to rescue him if he needed it.

Mark decided he was as calm as he was likely to get and opened the car door.

He hated that the smell of these people who hurt him so much still smelled like home. He thought they should smell like deceit and bigotry and all things evil, but they didn't. Yes, he had been kicked out, but no, he didn't wither and die or suffer daily with the gnashing of teeth. Nope, he studied hard and fast and passed his GED on the first try. He started community college 2 months after that and took more than full time credits while working as a busboy at a shitty buffet off the strip. Had he struggled before he was able to find help? Of course, but they didn't know that. They didn't know what he had to do before he found the person to help him get an identity and gave him a place to stay until he was able to get a start for himself, first by paying Tiny rent then by moving out and into his own small studio apartment. He was happier, mentally healthier, and so much stronger now than he had ever been in the pack.

Before he even had a chance to make it to the trunk of the car the front door of the lodge opened, and his former alpha stepped out.

"Boys, come help Mark with his things." The alpha

hollered. Mark could hear half a dozen footsteps running from around the back of the porch. The boys that ran toward him varied in age from about 8 to 15, but that was just Mark's guess.

Opening his trunk Mark handed bags and boxes to the boys with a smile. The alpha spoke up then. "Boys, take his things to the first cabin, the one I showed you." As they headed off the alpha stuck out his hand toward Mark. Mark wasn't sure what he made of that but shook his hand anyhow. "Directly behind the lodge is an A-frame that the owners lived in originally. It's a two bedroom with a large open kitchen living room area and it has a loft area that has a bedroom, small restroom, and a sitting room. The living room area will be changed to be more like a waiting area or whatever you think is best." The alpha sighed. "Sorry, I'm being overbearing. Being less of an alpha and more of a mayor is going to take some getting used to. Also, I know this isn't ideal for you and Alpha Mariam let me know that you will only be here for the duration of your vacation. But I do want this to be as comfortable for you as possible. Thank you for your time."

Mark looked straight into the man's eyes before answering. "This isn't for you. Alpha saved me. I was withering without a pack, and she organized us, giving us pack strength again. She accepted who and what I am. She valued my experience and education and told me I was worthy. I would do anything for her. And even after all that I told her 'no' when she asked if I would do this. That is how much I don't want to be here."

The alpha nodded sadly. "I understand. I deserve that. Thank you for coming anyway, to take care of the people that did you no harm. The innocent people that I was supposed to make sure were safe because they were in my care, and I failed, so again, thank you." He held out his hand, indicating to Mark the direction to head, to get to the A-frame apparently.

Mark looked around the campground and apparently the alpha was more perceptive than Mark gave him credit for. "They didn't come. They agreed with the others, I couldn't get them to see reason."

Mark was disappointed and felt a lump rising in his throat. Why did he think that suddenly his parents would want to be good people? He'd probably never see them again. He swallowed down the lump in his throat and sighed, moving toward the A-frame with more determination than he had just 30 seconds ago.

Bryce was correct in thinking that the A-frame would make a good medical office. "We will need to make a few changes to these two downstairs bedrooms to make them into procedure rooms. I would like one to be able to convert to a surgical room if and when it's needed."

Bryce scrubbed a hand across his face. "That sounds pricey."

"Don't worry," Mark sighed. "Alpha will make sure it happens." He continued around the cabin. "We will need to get a newer, better washer and dryer. And I think an autoclave will fit on this counter." He indicated a small counter that would be best described as a clothes folding table next to the existing ancient washer and dryer. He pulled out his phone and started making notes, quickly adding dishwasher to the list along with a slew of other basic medical necessities, including exam tables.

Currently the rooms each held a pair of twin beds that looked like they'd been sitting there since the 70's. Ew.

Bryce cleared his throat discreetly behind him, making Mark turn around to see what he wanted. "I know you just got here, and you haven't even settled where you'll be sleeping yet, but is there any way you can take a minute or two to look over a couple of the women? They're heavy with pups and both have been wincing since we started packing and not saying a word. I'm worried about them." Bryce's face was red, and he seemed embarrassed. "And I mean it, thank you, Mark. We did everything wrong with you and you are still here. I know you're here because Alpha Mariam asked, but I am very grateful nonetheless."

Mark sighed. "Sure. Let me grab my kit from the car and then you can show me to their cabins. This place isn't ready for anything yet and if they really are struggling, the less they walk the better."

The duo made their way back to Mark's rental car where he quickly grabbed his black leather bag, his name embossed in gold near the top. Bryce let out a whistle. "That is a nice bag, better than I've seen most doctors have." At first Mark thought Bryce was being condescending but when he looked at his face, he only saw honest admiration for his fine bag. "I was looking for something nice for our pack healer and I know how pricey they can be, especially if you count all the stuff you need in it as well."

Mark let loose his first smile. "When I graduated, I only knew two other shifters in the area, they were proud of me. Dave bought the bag, and Tiny filled it. Over the years as I've needed more things Alpha has bought them. I tried to pay for them myself and she wouldn't let me. She says as long as I'm the official pack emergency medic the pack will provide what I need."

Bryce smiled back a little sadly. "I wish I'd been a better Alpha to you. I let down a lot of people, not just you. I am hoping that I can find the ones who had to leave, invite them here or at least set them up with Alpha Mariam. I've kept good records, so I'm hoping Alpha will be able to help me track them down."

Mark wasn't ready to forgive the man, but he believed the words he was speaking. "If you show me the records, I can at least help you cross off the ones that are already in our pack. There are quite a few."

They made the short walk to a one room cabin that looked like all the rest from the outside. Bryce knocked on the door and a soft "Come in." sounded from inside. Bryce opened the door and ushered Mark ahead of him. "Oh, I'm sorry Alpha…would you like some tea? I could make some if you'd like." The woman started sitting up in the bed she'd been resting on.

"Don't be silly Bea, and I'm just Bryce now, not Alpha. I asked Mark to check on all of you that are expecting, the move was sudden and stressful, is it for my peace of mind if that's alright?"

The woman in question was tall, like most wolves, and a willowy thing except for her large belly that she currently had her hands around in a protective stance. She had an all american girl next door look, red hair and green eyes, a smattering of freckles across her nose and cheeks, her eyes stealing the attention from everything else in the room. "I'm fine Alph…Bryce. I don't need any special treatment."

Bryce smiled at the woman. "I'm sure you are but our

new Alpha went to the trouble of sending us some medical help, let's not take it for granted."

"I know how nerve wracking it can be to see someone new, I promise I won't do anything you don't want me to." Mark smiled at the young woman.

Finally, the woman nodded and rested back on the bed.

"When are you due?"

Mark asked all the important questions and took some notes. He measured her and listened to the fast little heartbeat of the pup. Tabitha liked that. "Is that him? My pup?"

Mark smiled. "Sure is. They sound strong and you look great. I think you need to rest for the next couple of days just to recover from the crazy, stressful move, but I think you'll be just fine. I would like to come and see you every week until the pups come though if that's alright with you?"

She seemed nervous but looked towards Bryce with a question in her eyes. He gave her a reassuring smile. "Alright. That would be fine I guess."

And so, the afternoon continued until the last visit. Unlike the other women this one was pregnant with multiples. She kept referring to the twins but when Mark listened to the heartbeats, he was pretty sure he heard three, and her stomach was contracting every so often. Hopefully just Braxton Hicks but Mark knew he needed to get the doctor here sooner rather than later.

"Everything sounds good Bea, but I'm going to double check when the doctor will be here. I'm worried these pups might make an early appearance. If it's ok with you I'm going to come back tomorrow just to make sure you're still doing alright?" She nodded and had a worried look about her. "Don't worry, we are going to make sure that you and your pups are in safe hands."

Bryce and Mark left the cabin and Mark immediately tried to call Joey. No signal. "Is there a phone I can use? I really need to find out when the doctor is going to be here."

"We have one in the main lodge. I'll show you."

3

"Do I know anyone in Wyoming?" Joey asked the empty office he was currently working in. "Hello?"

"Hey Joey, it's Mark."

"Oh! How is the campground?"

"There is no cell service, for starters." Mark chuckled. "I didn't realize how attached to my phone I am."

"I can't imagine going without mine for any real amount of time." Joey took a deep breath before continuing. "Are you doing alright? Being back with your old pack?"

Mark didn't answer immediately but finally sighed and spoke. "It's odd. Really odd. But I don't really want to talk about that right now, I'm still not ready to unpack all of what I'm feeling. I'm actually calling to see if you'd talked to Gemma."

"I did," Joey started. "she isn't too thrilled at the idea of going out that way. And before you ask, yes, I told her it was at the Alpha's request and that she was really needed.

She really didn't want to help. She was about to accept a new position in Hilo of all places. After I explained about what had happened and that there were so many people that needed a doctor in the pack she finally agreed to go. We are lucky she was already finished packing up her condo and was basically living out of her suitcase. Instead of shipping her stuff to Hilo she's going to get a truck and drive herself that way. She's leaving tomorrow."

Joey heard Mark let out a relieved sigh. "I am so happy to hear you say that. I have way too many pregnant women up here. Too much could go wrong. Especially the last one I saw today. She thinks she's having twins, but has never seen a real doctor, just the pack healer who didn't come along. I'm pretty sure it's triplets. And this move was sudden and hard, both emotionally and physically. This woman is about to go into labor. I really hope Gemma gets here on time. Do you happen to know if she's bringing any medical equipment with her?"

"I don't think she was planning on it. Why don't you give me the list of what you need, and I'll let Alpha know? We will get it to you as fast as we can."

The next few minutes were filled with list making and going over the details of what they needed Alpha Mariam to know and what they could do themselves to help and most importantly, getting the shopping list together for the medical center they wanted to put together.

When they finished going over all the boring details, they took some time to chat like friends do.

"So how is mated life treating you?" Joey could hear the smile in Mark's voice.

"I'm loving it. We still are working through a lot, my guilt, his anger, all justified feelings but not productive ones. I think we are handling everything well. It has helped a lot that both of us are really needed to work with and teach Mickey and Chris. Poor boys didn't realize what their relationship was, they're still a little confused sometimes, but at least we have them calling when things get confusing instead of holding it all in." He let out a small laugh. "We just have to tiptoe around the fact that their mate is Elkan's sister, it weirds him out sometimes. I think it's hilarious, don't tell him I said that."

"Poor guy, thinking about your baby sister as a mated adult must be hard for him."

"He'll survive. How long do you think you'll be up there once Gemma arrives? Will both of you be needed to set everything up?"

"I think once Gemma is here and somewhat settled that I can help her clean up and at least partially set up a med center in just a couple days. I really need to get away from here as fast as possible. It's not a comfortable place for me. And I'm feeling like I need to be home."

"Well, I will make sure and call Alpha Mariam right now and give her this information, then I'll call Gemma. She'll probably speed up her move once I tell her about the patients you've already seen. Be safe, ok? And call if you need anything else."

"I will. The only thing I need is to get home and visit the club."

They laughed and chatted a few more minutes before finishing the call. Joey did as he'd promised and made quick work of calling the Alpha and Gemma.

"Everything going well in Wyoming?" Joey smiled at the sound of his mate's voice.

"As well as we expected. We just need to get Mark

away from there as quickly as we can. He sounded stressed and I really can't blame him. He's taking care of people that shunned him. He's a professional and will do his job, but if he has to do it too long it's going to have an impact."

"Enough business talk. Let's go to the diner and get some food before I bring you back home and lock you in our bedroom."

4

---

*L*ess than 48 hours later Mark was making his way towards the loud moving truck making its way up the drive. It slowed down and came to a stop near the front of the main lodge. The truck turned off and the driver just sat there. Mark had to smile because he knew she was doing much the same as he had. Trying to muster the courage to open the door.

Finally, after two or three minutes the door opened, and Gemma stepped out. She was just as gorgeous as ever. Dark Auburn hair was pulled back into a ponytail on the back of her head, accentuating the slender face and wide mouth. She looked good, better than the last time Mark saw her. Her skin was glowing, and he could tell that she'd been lucky enough to have plenty of outdoor time. She was a little claustrophobic, so he was glad to see she had been enjoying the outdoors. She was tall, even for a shifter, about 6"1', and thin like a model. Mariam kept trying to fatten her up with cakes and baked goods, but the fact was that her genetics were just built that way.

"Hey Gemma, how was the drive?" He smiled and held out his hand.

Gemma gave him a firm handshake and a smile. "It was awful. My truck's AC went out and I didn't want to stop long enough for them to bring a replacement. But the air felt pretty good, actually it had been quite a long time since I'd driven down the highway singing songs and letting the wind whip my hair into knots."

"So, want to see the clinic?"

"Uh-oh, it's not like you to cut to the chase without at least a little small talk. I take it you're worried I need to get settled quickly because of a patient?"

"More like I'm worried you won't have time to even start getting settled. Let's walk while we talk." Mark indicated the way, much like Bryce had for him just two days ago. "All of the women were experiencing some signs of preterm labor. I put them on bedrest, and they seem to be fine, all but one. Her name is Bea and she's having triplets. She is nowhere near far enough along and I can't get her contractions to stop. They are still far apart and irregular, but she's started dilating. I'm worried."

Mark opened the screen door of the A frame and led Gemma in. Since he'd arrived, he'd worked as hard as he could to get this place as ready as possible. It smelled of paint fumes currently and he could hear at least three people working around the building. "We started with painting and checking the roof and plumbing. Fortunately, we have a lot of skilled laborers living here. The exam tables and autoclave as well as quite a bit of tools should be here today or tomorrow, Alpha paid a ton to get them here that quickly. The rest of the furniture will trickle in over the next couple of weeks. As soon as we were done painting, we sanded and polished the floors. So, the basic sanitation is done. There will be a lot more work needed to make one of these rooms into an emergency surgical suite, but Alpha agrees that we need it. There are just a lot of people here and the closest hospital is hours away."

Gemma had been silently listening to Mark. She interrupted when he finally took a breath. "Mark, it's ok. You're doing great but I don't expect a state-of-the-art facility in less than three days. I knew what I was walking into. Show me the upstairs, Alpha said that would be my living quarters, is that right?"

Mark smiled. "Yes, just until we can get a cabin put together for you. They're focusing on the elderly and pregnant families first then the rest. For now, about half of the people that came are sleeping on their mattresses in the main lodge. Fortunately, it has a large kitchen for them, and the weather is nice so the kids and everyone else can spend plenty of time outside during the day. They're rushing to get some more cabins built before the weather turns. Winter can be rough up here and they don't think they'll be able to do much once the snow hits.

He led her up the stairs to the small apartment-like area. "This is the sitting area or your living room slash office. This door leads to a good-sized bedroom with a nice bathroom, no tub but a nice shower." He held open the door to show her the inside of the restroom. "I'm not sure why they thought this particular shade of pink was good for the basin, toilet and shower, all I can do is apologize." They both chuckled. "They have a lot of people with little to do until the cabins are put together, people that have no building experience. Those people have a chore rotation and they've added cleaning up the clinic and some light cleaning up here. When they come the first time you can let them know what not to touch etc.,"

"Thanks Mark, I appreciate how much you're doing to make this less difficult for me. Let's make some coffee downstairs and you can show me the files you've started. Bring me up to speed. Please let Bryce know that I don't need a different cabin, save those for the people that do. Upstairs will suit me just fine.

" The duo ended up sitting at the small breakfast bar drinking coffee from utilitarian white mugs that were in the cupboard already. "I can see why you're so concerned. I'll want to check on Bea and the others myself, but I am also worried about Bea. Triplets are rough and they rarely wait until full term. I think we need some more supplies. Alpha said I could call her with whatever I need, so I will. Can you give me a moment and then you can introduce me to the patients you've met?"

Mark nodded and then sat and sipped his coffee while Gemma called the Alpha. Mark wasn't paying too much attention, busy thinking about getting home and the plans he had when he got there. Before he knew it, he heard Gemma wrapping up the call. "…thank you again, and I'm grateful for the supplies you can get here. Mark was right to be worried." She smiled over at Mark. "Alright, thank you Alpha. I'll be ready for the supplies and equipment when it gets here."

She ended the call and sighed. "Alright, time to get to work. Introduce me." Mark set his mug down and smiled at Gemma. "They are actually very nice. I have a little bit of personal bias, but if I didn't then I would say that this is a wonderful little pack. Yes, yes, I'm aware they're part of our pack now, but you know what I mean."

They started towards the cabins and Mark gave a running commentary, pointing out things of interest, like the trail to the lake and the trail that led to the large campfire area behind the main lodge, where most meetings would be held while the weather was still good. "Then eventually when the mass of people in the main lodge have their own cabins the lodge will be where the pack meetings are during the winter months. It's way too cold for outdoor meetings in winter, especially for the little ones."

They made their way through the list of women that were pregnant and much like Mark suspected they were all starting to feel themselves again, all except Bea. Her contractions were getting closer and more regular. Still not too close but it wouldn't be more than a couple of days before these pups made their way into the world. When all the introductions were made, they started back towards the medical clinic. Mark was surprised to see a group of men clearing a large spot behind the main lodge and lining the edges with rocks that had been painted white. He was a little confused until he heard Bryce's voice booming from a distance. "Hey Mark, Dr Gemma, nice to finally meet you. I think we are just about done so the helicopter shouldn't have any problems landing. We did it just like he told us to."

Mark's face must've looked as confused as he felt because he heard Gemma laugh before she spoke. "Alpha Mariam said that one of her brothers-in-law flew the helicopter for the family business. When I told her how desperate we were for the equipment she promised to get it here via helicopter and had the pilot talk to Bryce about the requirements for making a nice place for him to land. Looks like I'll have the things I need some time tomorrow. The closest airport would add a full day to the trip. I don't think we have an extra 24 hours."

"Which brother?" Mark asked, then blushed.

Gemma laughed, "Why? Which one has your eye?"

"I just like looking, they are lacking what I really want but they are all very pretty."

~

*E*veryone met outside of the lodge where they had dragged all the picnic tables from the grounds. A large meal had been made and was being served cafeteria style. Simple hamburgers, potato salad, and coleslaw. At least that's what Mark thought until he bit into the burger. "Oh my gosh. What is this?"

Bryce's wife was serving and giggled. "While we were clearing the trails and such, we found an Elk, the poor animal had a broken back leg. We put it out of its misery and made use of the meat. Mixed it up with the ground beef we'd bought in town. Added some diced-up bacon too. We love meat."

Mark moaned. "You've ruined me for all other burgers." Now Gemma was laughing at him too.

They finished their delicious meals and brought their dishes to the kitchen and put them in the tubs to be cleaned.

"How long do you think you need me to stay around?" Mark tried to sound nonchalant, but he knew he didn't succeed.

"Can you help me until Bea has the triplets? Then I should be alright on my own. I think it's going to be hectic when they come. It might also be dangerous, in fact that is what I'm assuming."

"Sounds good. I was thinking the same thing, those pups aren't waiting very much longer."

Mark walked Gemma back to the clinic. "Would you like to come in for some tea? You'd be doing me a favor, I held off my nervousness until I was done with the important stuff, now I need some distraction so I can relax." Gemma blushed at the confession.

Mark smiled. "Sure thing, we can exchange horror stories."

Gemma filled an electric kettle and started it. "I hope you like this tea." She grabbed a mason jar filled with an interesting looking tea in it. She continued speaking while she scooped out a fair amount and added it to the bottom of her French Press. "It's an Irish Pu Erh from this little local shop in Albuquerque. I found it last time I went to visit my cousin, Roslee. I can't get enough of it. If I had all my things unpacked, I'd make it a latte for you. Even without that, it's delicious."

Instead of sitting at the breakfast bar they took their cups to the small old couch that would soon be replaced and made themselves comfortable.

"You're right, this is delicious." Mark commented after sipping his tea.

"So do you hate being here as much as I do?" Gemma asked bluntly.

"HA! Yes. Yes, I do." He took a sip of the tea and sighed. "Do you want to talk about it?" At her look of apprehension, he added. "I'll show you mine if you show me yours?"

Now it was Gemma who laughed. "Sure." She folded herself more into the couch and took a breath. "Well, I'm a pariah. My father is a wolf, and my mother isn't. So, I was never accepted. We lived with my father's pack, even after he died."

"I'm so sorry."

"Thank you, it was over 20 years ago. I miss him but I'm ok. Well, after he died, we wanted to go live with my mother and her family, but they wouldn't take us back. She was tainted in their eyes. So, we stayed in Dad's pack. They gave us the worst house. The roof leaked, the furnace was broken, the insulation was practically nonexistent. In winter we had to sleep together in the living room because it was the only room with a fireplace. We'd drag our mattresses down and move the couch into the kitchen. It was ridiculous, but it worked. We were together. Then mom got sick. The pack healer refused to help an outsider. By the time we made it to a real doctor it was too late. She was too sick. All of it could have been prevented with just an ounce of compassion. She got sick from a stupid cut on her foot. We were breaking up old pallets for firewood and she stepped on a nail. She hid it from me and ended up with blood poisoning." Gemma seemed to need a moment and took a sip of her tea. "Well, I decided that I hated them all. My father's pack. My mom's pride. All of them. I don't belong anywhere, so I went to medical school and became a doctor. I vowed to help anyone who needed it, but I also vowed I'd never belong to a pack. So, here I am, doing a favor for the Alpha and wishing I could just get back to my old life but knowing I won't because I'd do anything the Alpha needed. She saved me. Because even if I'm just a half wolf, I need a pack." She paused again and looked into Mark's eyes. "You know how it is."

Mark nodded and took a moment to gather his thoughts. "This is my birth pack. Well, some of them. They had the choice to stay in Ohio and be the same way they've been for ages, bigoted and cruel, or to accept everyone and move here for a new start. My family didn't come. It's hard to forgive the old Alpha, mayor, whatever his new title is. But I've also been working with Alpha Mariam for so long to figure out what the hell is going on with the attacks and all the horror that comes with it. You've been helping as well, right?"

Gemma nodded. "Analyzing blood work and recently some tissue samples."

"Well, apparently the old Alpha and his wife have kept meticulous records and it's been very useful to try to figure some things out. So, I'm supposed to play nice. It's not easy. They kicked me out without even a high school diploma to help me. I found an underground network in Vegas that helped me. Dave and Tiny set me up with an identity that would hold up and helped me find a job. Tiny even helped me find scholarships and grants so I could afford school. Nursing school was what I wanted. People always assume I wanted to be a doctor and settled, but that's not the case. I always wanted to be a nurse. I'm happy in that role."

They were both silent for a minute before Gemma spoke again. "I take it your family will likely never accept you or the new pack dynamics?"

"Never. They are ignorant and stubborn. Until the day

I die I will never understand people who don't love their children. I'm dead to them. They tell people I'm dead or don't mention me at all. They would rather me be dead than gay. I'll never understand it, but at least I found my true Alpha and purpose. I know we are going to figure out all the weird stuff going on with these attacks. No one else has cared until Alpha Mariam. I think the gods sent her to us."

They let the heavy conversation fade away and enjoyed the rest of their tea.

"So," Mark started. "your space is upstairs. I'm staying in the next cabin over. Directly to the right when you step out the front door. I want to be close enough for an emergency and I'm not staying long enough to be assigned something better. I'd rather eat glass than huddle in with everyone in the main lodge. Hopefully I will be gone before I need to figure out a better sleeping arrangement. I'm anxious to get home. In fact, I feel like I'm being pulled there. It's odd."

They rinsed out their mugs and said goodnight.

The bed Mark was trying to sleep on was old and lumpy, but the others helping had tried their best to pound the dust out of it and make it as clean as possible in the room. He appreciated their efforts even if the bed was killing his back. It took a little longer than usual but eventually Mark faded into sleep.

5

----

*D*aniel was grateful for the break. He'd moved out of the family house ages ago, but they always got together at least once a week for a run and dinner. Mom insisted. It had never really bothered him before but now with everyone magically finding their mates, and him left in the cold watching the affection, well, it was making him a little grumpy. Even his baby sisters had found their mates. At least with Adam's new pups his mom might stop pestering them all for grand-kids. Regardless, the small trip to drop off supplies was a grateful reprieve.

The air had been perfect and the flight flawless. He saw the clearing they'd prepared easily and landed with the grace that a couple decades of experience gave him. As soon as everything was powered down and safe, he saw Mark and a group of young men making their way over to him.

"Hello again." Daniel said, waving at Mark. He'd only briefly met Mark, but he seemed like a good sort. Maybe a little sad but always smiling. "You here to make sure I don't break all this shiny stuff while unloading it.?" He spoke the words with a smile on his face.

Mark laughed. "Yep, that's me, overseer of all things shiny."

The group made quick work of unloading the cellophane wrapped equipment and getting it over to the medical cabin. When everything was carried in Mark quickly dismissed the young men that had helped.

"I see you looking at me," Mark smiled. "before you take off, I'd love some help getting all of this unwrapped and sanitized. I know Airplane work isn't the same as medical work, but unlike the young men that helped us unload, I know that you're used to handling delicate equipment and paying attention to detail."

"How could you possibly know that?"

"You haven't fallen out of the sky yet. And Elkan told me you do all your own repairs and maintenance on the helicopter. So, I know you won't muck up these incubators but actually be helpful. I am sorry to ask, but the doctor, Gemma, is with Bea right now and we don't think she'll be able to keep those pups in for much longer, as in she wants this room ready ASAP."

"Tell me what to do and I'll get it done. Mariam asked if I'd be willing to stay a couple of days to help you get everything settled so we could get you home sooner." Daniel wasn't surprised to see a wave of relief flash across Mark's face.

"Thank you."

They spent the next couple of hours getting everything set up in the room Gemma chose as Exam Room 2.

"Hey," Daniel's voice startled Mark from his reading.

The neonatal equipment was the newest and top of the line and Mark had spent the last few minutes reading the actual manual, with a smile on his face. "Why would the Doc ask for the last room to be fixed up first? Why not the room we just passed, 'Exam 1'?"

Mark sat down the book he was reading and reached for his water bottle, taking a drink before answering. "The triplets aren't going to wait so we need the surgical suite, or 'Exam 2' to be ready. The other room is for most everything, but not surgery, while this room will be able to do both emergencies and run of the mill stuff, hopefully by tonight. And the reason she picked the rear room instead of the front for that is a couple different reasons, firstly, there are six outlets in this room while the other only had two, secondly, the location provides for a more sterile environment when and if it is needed as a surgical suite."

I nodded my head and reached for my own bottle of water. "Got it. You really think we will have this ready tonight?"

"Sure. We have the new bed set up, both incubators ready, cleaned and prepped, and the OB kit is sterilizing as we speak in that amazing new autoclave, we hooked up next to the washer and you just finished setting up the lights. We cleaned the room top to bottom and when we are finished, I'll do the floors again. It's not perfect, not sterile enough by far if it wasn't for our healing abilities, but it's way more than any other pack I've ever known to have."

"Where is the doctor? I still haven't met her."

"I know she was going to check in on Bea, the woman

we are rushing to set up for, and then she needed to check on one of the older women who hurt herself in the move." Mark took another drink from his water and continued. "I am not too sure what time she'll be back, but hopefully, we set this all up to her liking."

Daniel gave Mark a smile. "Me too, I really don't want to be asked to move it all again." They both chuckled.

$\sim$

*M*ark and Daniel finished up and with an enormous yawn Mark waved a farewell and left.

Daniel looked around the clinic and sighed. In the hustle and bustle of the day he'd forgotten to check if they had a place for him to sleep. He knew the Doctor was going to be sleeping upstairs and he had no desire to encroach into her personal space, so he set himself to the task of finding some blankets, the ratty looking couch was going to have to do. He finally found a stack of gorgeous, if not a little old, quilts in a small closet in the hall. He knew from watching his mom work that these quilts were not only beautiful but difficult to make. Someone very skilled had spent time outfitting this campground.

Daniel grabbed a beautiful quilt with a wheel pattern on it. He didn't know what this pattern was called, but his mom would. He just knew that the material seemed soft as butter and gave off a sense of comfort. He made his way to the old but functional couch and spread out the quilt. He was getting tired fast. He made quick work of removing his clothes, right down to his overpriced boxer briefs that his last lover insisted he have. He shook his head remembering the ridiculous amount of money he paid for underwear. He made himself comfortable and was out before his head hit the pillow.

aniel jumped out of bed and wasn't sure why at first, then a second knock on the door reminded him. He rushed to the door and opened it to find a man holding an extremely pregnant woman in his arms. "The doctor, we need the doctor!" The man's eyes were wide with adrenaline and worry.

"I'll be right down! Go to Exam 2!" Daniel wasn't sure when she'd come home but he'd obviously been asleep. He held the door wide and indicated the way to the room. The man came in and headed the way indicated while Daniel closed the door behind him. Crap. He knew it wasn't the right time, but one of those two were his mate.

Not long after the duo arrived, Mark came running over from wherever he'd been sleeping, he was a little out of breath but didn't stop to do anything but wash his hands before quickly making his way into the room the gorgeous man had taken the beautiful woman into. He really hoped they weren't mates. That would complicate matters greatly, considering one of them was his. Along with Mark was another young lady who had her own baby bump. She looked as worried as the others had.

As if on cue, his life became even more messy. The doctor came running down the stairs in full scrubs, ready for whatever awaited her in the exam room. How could he have not realized until just now that the doctor was also his mate? Daniel shrugged; his mother would be thrilled. As soon as the doctor, Gemma, was close to him, her steps faltered for just a beat. Her head whipped to the side, looking towards him. "Well shit."

Not the wonderful welcome he was expecting from his mate, but he couldn't blame her., She was busy.

"Later." he told her with a small nod. She nodded back and took off yet again.

7

*D*aniel didn't know if he was losing his mind or if this is what people always felt like when they found their mates. All he knew was they were trying their best to save four lives right now and he just wanted them all to himself. It made him feel a little like an asshole. He really hoped that he was feeling this way because it was all so new and he still needed to claim them, and not that he would feel this way every single time someone else needed their attention. His mom was a doctor, and his dad didn't seem to lose a shit every time she was on a call. So, he was optimistic.

He was still feeling a bit of a shock about everything when the young man who carried the woman in came out of the room. Well, his first question was answered. That was his mate.

"Do you know where I'd find a cup of ice chips?? Mark told me to ask you. My sister is dying of thirst." And the second question was answered too. Not mates. He quickly grabbed a Styrofoam cup he'd seen in a cupboard earlier and opened the freezer.

"Grab a spoon out of that drawer there." Daniel walked to the door next to where his mate was waiting. The man grabbed his spoon, pausing a little when he took the cup from Daniel.

"How is this going to work? I was surprised when Doc Gemma came in and I found that the great doctor for our pack was also my mate... Now this." He used his free hand to indicate the two of them.

"We will figure it out, later, go help your sister. I'll be here when you're done." He smiled. "I'm Daniel by the way." The man smiled back.

"Hi Daniel, I'm Kyle." With that, he headed back to the room.

He made himself sit back down on the couch to relax for a while, or at least pretend to. Occasionally his mate would run out of one room into the other to grab something they obviously needed. He had yet to make eye contact with Kyle since they spoke that first time. Daniel did his best to try and rest a little more while he waited. When that didn't work, he got up and made a fresh pot of coffee. He had found the coffee pot earlier when he was looking for blankets. He had just sat down with his own cup of coffee when Mark walked out of the room looking haggard.

"How's it going?"

Mark scrubbed a hand down his face before answering. "Done. Three healthy pups. 2 girls and a little boy. They're little, but after a day or two they should be fine. For now, they'll stay here, thank goodness for healing abilities and how fast our pups grow at first. They wouldn't have made it if they weren't wolves."

Daniel nodded "Good. My mom always said that our healing makes her job easier." Mark chuckled at that and rubbed his hand across his eyes.

"That's true. I'm heading out, I think I'll sleep in tomorrow and then head home." he stretched his back first, one way than the other. "I'm going to get myself all gussied up and spend some time at your brother's club. How I've been a member for as long as I have without visiting is insane. I'm really starting to feel it."

Daniel smiled. Very few people knew his brother was one of the owners of the newest shifter BDSM club in Nevada. It worked out great for him and from what he understood, Elkan, along with his mate Joey, have been mentoring for Christian and Mickey as well as just playing.

"How gussied up are we talking?" he waggled his eyebrows in an exaggerated flirty way. It worked to make Mark laugh. Which was what he had been trying to do.

"I finally decided to dye my hair for starters, and I'm thinking about a manicure and pedicure too. I haven't had time to do anything for myself in quite a while.

Mark seemed to be waiting for judgment of some sort. He'd have to be a lot more shocking for that to happen. "I recommend Willie, Wilhelmina, I'll text you her info. She does hair too, but I use her for my manicures. Working on choppers is a little greasy, not the smooth sexy look I'm usually aiming for."

Mark smiled. "Thanks, I would appreciate that. I called a place that got all weirded out when I tried to make an appointment. I mean, it's not like it's 1920, a manicure shouldn't be scandalous. People are odd."

The two men fell into silence while they drank some coffee. Finally with an enormous yawn, Mark made his way to the door. With the silent wave over his shoulder to Daniel he left.

Daniel could still hear the doctor talking to the new mother and Kyle and the young lady that came in with them, he never caught her name. He was about to give up and go back to bed when the doctor and Kyle quietly made their way out of the room. Kyle left the door cracked a bit before turning towards the other two. Gemma seemed agitated and was pacing the living room. Daniel looked questioningly at Kyle, who simply shrugged his shoulders and the universal "I don't know" sign. Finally, Gemma stopped pacing. She looked at them and sighed.

"You two. Follow me." She turned and made her way up the stairs. Daniel didn't think it would be the last time they would do whatever she asked of them.

8

How could this be happening? She did not want a single mate, let alone two. She didn't get any other wolf traits, so why this one period, shit.

The two men followed her up the stairs and now stood in the small loft area that held a small loveseat and her office boxes, which she'd unpack eventually. Damn it. They were really cute. Kyle looks so much like his sister, with dark skin and tight braids hanging artfully around his face. And eyes so deep brown that it felt like you could swim in them. In stark difference was Daniel. He had sandy brown hair, tan skin that showed he was probably of mixed heritage somewhere and eyes a deep green like the trees in late summer. They both stood about 6 foot five, but where Daniel had broad shoulders that tapered to a tight waist like a swimmer, Kyle looked long and sleek., like he should be running marathons in his spare time. How could these be her mates?

"Sit" she pointed to the love seat. After a couple of false starts, she was able to manage a sentence. "I'm not sure how this works. Do we all feel attraction to each other? Do you two want to be together? Also? Are you both bi? What? I'm so out of my element."

The two men in question looked at each other and came to some type of agreement, and Kyle spoke up. "Yeah, we all feel it. I've never been with a man, didn't consider myself bi, but I'm not anti, it's just never come up." he looked towards Daniel who continued.

"I'm pan. I've never cared about gender or sex or whatever, If I like a person then I just liked them."

That was interesting. "So, this isn't a problem for you?" Gemma asked. "you've been with men before?"

Daniel nodded his head. "Men, women, and non-binary as well. Honestly, I'm Demi. I just want a connection. The most disturbing thing to me tonight is that I have a desire to jump both of you and claim you and I don't even really know you. That's very unlike me."

Gemma nodded. "OK, that makes sense. I think you should know something about me before you get too excited. You both got stuck with a dud. I'm only half wolf. My dad. My mom was a shifter too but not a wolf. It's a sore spot for me. Dad's pack refused to believe there were any kind of other shifters. Even after seeing my mom in her lion form. When Dad died. I went with my mom back to the pride, but her family wanted her to leave me with the pack. She was welcome and I wasn't. Because she chose to keep me, they exiled us to the outer edges of the pack which eventually killed her, period, no one else to blame for her death. I can shift, that's a secret, both the pack and clowder claimed it was impossible. I am a cat. Specifically, a lion. I don't know if I'll ever be able to have children, there is very little medical info on mixed kids."

Daniel and Kyle were both quiet for a beat. Finally, Kyle spoke up. "I didn't know there were other shifters. Makes sense though. If you can't have kids, then we will figure that out. If nothing else, we have three pups downstairs to spoil for a while."

Daniel jumped in. "not to mention my brand-new nieces' back home in Oregon, and a couple more pups coming any day now to my little sister. I don't like to think about that though, the twins are too young to be starting families, but I guess the stupid crazy illness you've been doing research on for Mariam doesn't care about age."

Gemma grimaced, "I'm sorry. Was she hurt too badly?"

Daniel shook his head inside. "Actually, her mates seemed to be taking it worse than she has. They've been thick as thieves since they were pups. It hit the three of them all at once, regrets are high, the boys actually ran away because they felt so much guilt about what happened. They're all back together again and my sister's twin found her mate also, one of them, at least. The three boys are sharing the duplex that they will eventually share with the girls. Mom and Dad are insisting they wait till they're 18. All of them. It's going to be tricky, but I agree with my parents on that. They are very young." Daniel paused for a moment. "Sorry, I got sidetracked there."

"That's alright, it distracted me for a while too." sighing again, Gemma continued. "So, I do have some issues. You both should know about it before we go any further."

"We don't want to rush you." Kyle's words seemed genuine, but she laughed. A mirthless laugh.

"I think we all know we're barely holding on as is, I

don't see us waiting much longer." She sighed again. "I can't be held down by my shoulders. I don't mind a little bit of play, but I need to know in my brain that I can move away if I want to. Wrists are OK, hips, whatever, but if you hold down my shoulders I will probably attack. What should I know about you two?"

"If we're talking about lifestyle stuff. We need a much deeper conversation," Daniel began. "but for tonight we just need to keep it vaguely vanilla. I think."

Kyle chuckled. "Since I don't even know what he means when he says lifestyle, I will assume vanilla is my flavor. Just, I, I've never been with a man before." Kyle turned his gaze to Daniel. "If we do anything, which I know my wolf is wanting, I'm hoping you'll take it easy and give me lots of pointers, I don't know what the hell I'm doing. You should both know that I'm not a huge fan of sex. I think I'm some sort of Ace spectrum, but nobody has hung around long enough for me to figure out myself."

Daniel smiled and brought his hand up to Kyles's cheek softly, he spoke, "I promise. I have no desire to hurt you, or me, I want to show you nothing but pleasure." he leaned in and gave a sweet soft kiss, just a small brush of lips really, and smiled "Promise."

Gemma had to swallow before she could speak. "Well, since that was way hotter than I thought it would be, I propose we move this to my bedroom. Which is going to need a king size bed soon, the Queen is going to be squishy. I made sure we could be here if she calls for us, but she should be pretty exhausted, Same with the pups."

All three walked into the bedroom. Gemma stood near the edge of the bed and reached a hand out to Kyle and Daniel. They didn't make her wait but walked to her and took the hands she offered. She brought them closer and wrapped her arms around both men. She was so happy when they did the same. All three of them held each other for a brief time, the calm before the storm. "Kyle, before I lose control of my desire, I want to make sure you're ok with everything that is happening. I don't want you to feel pressured into having sex with us. I don't know what it's like to be in a relationship with someone that is ace so I'm going to need you to be very open with me. With us. I can't read your mind so I will always ask for the words."

Kyle smiled down at her. "I will tell you to stop if I am uncomfortable or don't want something. But as of right now my wolf is spurring me on. I want you and I want Daniel. I don't know how long my desire for sex will last, it might stay now that I've found my mates, but more likely I will go back to how I've always been once my wolf is satisfied with our mating and claiming. I hope that you will understand that if I don't want to have sex with you in the future that it in no way means that I don't care for you. You are my mate, and I will always care for you." He turned his head, making eye contact with Daniel. "And you. I will always want to be with you both."

Daniel leaned down, giving another kiss to Kyle. It started slow and sweet but had all three of them panting and wanting before they were done.

"If you might not want to do this again then I'd like to request that you make love to both of us tonight. Sate your wolf and let us feel claimed. I don't know about Gemma, but I do know that my wolf won't be satisfied until I've made love to you. Is that something you can do for me? Or am I asking too much?" Daniel blushed at his request.

Kyle smiled and nodded. "I would love to be with both of you tonight. You are right, I might not want this again. Let's take advantage of our wolves' impatience."

It no longer felt like they were in a frenzied hurry. It was as if all of them knew that this claiming was special and something to be cherished. They lay in the bed kissing and petting each other and learning each other's bodies. Gemma was looking up at Kyle and stopped kissing him just long enough to speak. "Even if you don't want to have sex with us, will you always stay with us? Sleep with us and hold us?"

"Forever."

But not tonight. Tonight was for claiming. Kyle looked to Daniel, spread out on his side, his long body snug to the side of Gemma's. "Kiss me mate." Daniel smiled and leaned in. Kyle took the initiative in their kiss, which was a beautiful thing to see. Gemma watched them from beneath Kyle's body. Soon they were all moving together, writhing, and touching each other as much as they could.

It was a long while before they fell asleep. Gemma and Daniel had both been thoroughly claimed by Kyle and he had watched and touched and kissed while Gemma and Daniel made love to each other over and over again.

9

$\mathcal{M}$orning came early, much earlier than Mark would've liked. He blinked his eyes open and stretched his body until it popped and cracked. It felt great. Not as great as it would've been if he'd slept in his own bed, but he'd take all the rest he could get after last night. He made quick work of getting ready for the day and packing up the few things he brought with him. He couldn't wait to get away from this place. Just as he was thinking he might manage to get on the road without having to talk to anyone, there was a light knocking on the door. Mark sighed at his bad luck but walked to the door and opened it, nonetheless.

"Morning." There stood the last person he wanted to see. Bryce. The mayor.

"Good morning, Bryce. I was just about to take off, what can I help you with?" Mark knew he was being a little rude, but honestly, he was done with being nice and he wanted to go home. He felt like he needed to be there as soon as possible.

Bryce looked a little sheepish and like he was out of his element, but he stood there anyways and, taking a deep breath, started speaking. "I am glad I caught you before you left. I wanted to tell you how sorry I am." Mark took a breath to speak, but before he could say anything Bryce continued. "I know the words aren't enough. I don't ever expect you to forgive me, that's not what I'm here for, and honestly, I don't really know if you should forgive me. I was your alpha, and I didn't take care of you. That was my job and I failed you. I failed quite a few of you, truth be told. I want you to know that I'm different now. You don't have to believe me or anything like that, but I wanted you to know. I made so many mistakes trying to hold the old pack together and there was no reason to. I should've taken the good eggs and made my way here years ago. Instead, I turned a blind eye to so many things. I don't think I even wanted to know what was really going on. I know that's wrong, and really shows that I wasn't ready to oversee a pack. Things are going to be different here. Everyone will be welcome here. And anybody who treats anybody else with discrimination or bigotry will have to leave. I'm lucky enough to have a mate to tell me when I was wrong and what I was wrong about. So, I'm not asking for your forgiveness. I probably never will. I just want you to know that I'm sorry. And I want you to know that the alpha can trust me with taking care of anybody she needs to send my way. Anyone. Anytime. No matter what. This is a sanctuary." Bryce didn't wait for a response, just gave a nod of his head, and turned to leave with "Get home safely." Over his shoulder.

Mark stared at the closed door long after Bryce walked through it. He wasn't sure what he should've said, if anything. Finally, he decided that it was just too much to think about right now and, picking up his duffle, made his way to the car.

~

Mark had been driving for an hour or so when his phone rang. He smiled when he saw who it was. "Hey Dave, what's up?"

Dave had been a good friend for more years than Mark wanted to admit, he was one of the first people he'd met when he moved to Nevada. Dave and Tiny had been running a secret rescue mission of sorts for years before Mariam had suggested they work together and form the Hidden Pack. After Mark joined them, he added a professional medical element and helped them find a lot more people that needed their help. If a shifter had to come in for a break or concussion, it was way worse than most people could imagine.

"Hey, I thought you would be back already, but I drove by your house, and you weren't there. I was hoping we could use your spare room, just for the night. Our other safehouse already has a resident tonight." Dave sounded a little desperate.

"Sure, just use your key to let them in. Make sure my room is locked though please, none of my stuff is put away and I don't want to traumatize anybody." Fortunately, Dave had seen all the stuff Mark wanted out of sight. While they didn't talk about it often, there had been a period when he and Dave had tried to give romance a go. While they enjoyed their time together, they mutually decided that there was something missing. They went back to being just friends without any problems or issues. There had been a few times since then that they had gone together to clubs, before Dave opened the new one, and they never had any friendship difficulties.

"Sounds good. You don't have a landline any longer do you?"

"No, however there is an old cell phone on a charger in the guest room so they can call 911 if they need to. I should be home tonight, let them know that. What can I expect when I get there?"

"Father and his two young kids. His wife was taken out by their alpha. Apparently, she let her alpha tendencies slip. He had thought the entire family were betas, she'd been hiding her alpha status her entire life right up until a comment was made about their son liking to wear his cousins hand me down princess dresses. Her eyes flashed red right there in front of the pack alpha who didn't notice but his young daughter did and mentioned it." Dave sounded tired.

"I will never understand the antiquated way some packs kick out or even kill all the alphas. It's ridiculous. Why wouldn't you want the strongest pack possible." Mark sighed. "Just let them in. The freezer is stocked with frozen dinners, all sorts, even the kid ones, and some steamer veggies, let them know to make themselves at home. Make sure they know that I'm coming in tonight, I would hate to scare them.

yle wasn't sure of the proper morning after protocol. Kyle wasn't a virgin, but he also wasn't as free loving as a lot of people now seemed to be. He could still count all the people he'd ever been with on one hand. Including last night. He wasn't embarrassed by the fact that he had only had two lovers in his life before meeting his mates, but it did make him feel a little insecure. For all he knew he was terrible in bed, and no one had ever mentioned it because they were trying to be nice. His sister Bea had always told him that sex wasn't something you scored like gymnastics or diving, it was something that got better with time because your affection for your partner grew and made it more and more special. Of course, he had also heard her and her best friend, Tabitha, talk about how good some guys were and how bad some others were. So, he was pretty sure she was just giving her obligatory sister support to him.

He had taken some time recently to look some things up online. He understood he was ace, but he didn't know what that would mean for their future. He could tell from his breathing that Daniel had woken up and was just playing possum. Should he talk to one without the other? How does this work? Before he could stress himself out any more than he already was he felt Daniel tap his shoulder lightly. He looked up at his mate's face and gave an awkward smile. Daniel scrunched his brow a little then cocked his head towards the door and started to carefully maneuver his way off the too small bed. Kyle followed.

They quietly made their way to the kitchen where Kyle took a seat on one of the barstools and watched Daniel start a pot of coffee. His mate stood in the kitchen in nothing but pride underwear and a grin. How did he feel so comfortable already? Kyle was suddenly feeling a little self-conscious of his body. He had barely enough chest hair to even be noticed, unlike Daniel who had a gorgeous mat of dark curls on his chest and trailing down his taut stomach before disappearing into that ridiculously cute underwear. Kyle sighed at the sight. As soon as he did, he wanted to take it back, because Daniel quickly turned to give him a knowing smile. His mate could see something was wrong though, even while Kyle tried to hide it. The adorable smile that Daniel gave him quickly turned to a look of concern.

Daniel finished what he was doing and hit start on the coffee maker. He rinsed his hands, drying them on a clean dish towel, and made his way around the counter to where Kyle was sitting. Kyle could feel the warmth of his body and it made him nervous. Daniel reached down and turned Kyle's barstool so that the two men were facing each other. He brought up his right hand and softly rubbed his fingers across Kyle's frowning brow.

"Why are you not as happy as me? Did you not want a mate?" Daniel asked the second question with a near whispered voice.

"That's not it." Kyle wanted to ease his mate's mind. "I didn't know if someone like me could get a true mate."

It was Daniel's turn to frown. "What do you mean by someone like you?"

Kyle knew he wanted to be honest, but it still took him a few tries to get the words out. "I have always heard of mating as this amazing physical connection and the almost impossible and overwhelming need to make love to your mate, and that you experience it almost all the time." He looked into Daniel's eyes for confirmation that he was following along. "But I'm ace, at least I thought I was. I thought I might never want someone like that, or with that amount of fervor, so maybe, maybe I wouldn't get a mate, fate wouldn't waste one on me."

Daniel bent down and kissed Kyle softly at his temple. "Is that all? I know plenty of people who are ace, and they are all waiting patiently for their true mate. And just so you know, if all true mates could think of nothing but having sex all day long, well, we wouldn't have anyone able to keep a job, or function at all really. Yes, we felt attraction last night and we didn't even question that our bodies wanted us to claim each other. But that won't always feel that strong." Daniel suddenly got a horrified look on his face. "You did WANT to be with us last night, right, you didn't just do it because you thought we'd expect it?"

"NO! I mean, yes, I wanted everything last night. It shocked me how much I wanted you both. And I enjoyed every moment. But what if it doesn't last? What if I rarely want to have sex? Will you both start to feel like you have a dud for a mate? I know I said some of this last night and now I'm just repeating myself, but it's rattling around in my head."

Before Daniel could answer a voice came from the stairs. "I will never think of you as a dud." Gemma made her way towards them wearing a short floral kimono type of robe that covered the pajama short set she had on. She looked beautiful. "If you treat me with respect and dignity, then you are doing everything I consider crucial for our mating to be successful. Eventually I'd like our mating to be filled with love. That doesn't have to be a physical relationship. But just to clear the air and be totally honest... I loved being with you and would welcome any sexy times with you."

Daniel nodded his head in agreement. "I agree with everything she just said. Every person in this world is different and unique. That means that there are no two matings that are identical. So, what we need in our relationship is different from what any other person needs from theirs. Does that make sense?'

Kyle nodded. "I'm just feeling a little insecure. I know I'm the baby in this relationship, but even with that I think I'd be feeling better if I felt like I knew what I was doing last night. I feel like you two really know what you like and how to please others, and I'm sitting there with only two previous lovers under my belt. And I only slept with them a few times. I just am feeling like I was a bad choice for having two mates."

Daniel spoke quietly but firmly. "You are not a bad choice. You were the person fate had in store for us. There is no such thing as a dud true mate. We will all find our place in this relationship. Whatever else we are, we are also a perfect fit." Daniel opened his arms and waited. He didn't rush or demand, just waited. Kyle made his way into his arms and rested his head on Daniel's shoulder while absorbing all the pure and honest emotion coming from the man. He felt so lucky to have such a wonderful mate as Daniel. Before he could say as much, he felt two feminine and strong arms coming around him from the back. He was cocooned in-between his mates and knew that he was exactly where he was supposed to be.

"Kyle?" His sister's voice startled him, but neither of his mates seemed inclined to let go of him. He turned his face, now blushing, toward his sister who stood at the entrance to the hallway, a look of shock on her face. "What's going on?"

Before he could answer he felt Gemma speak as she let go and walked toward Bea. "You should still be resting Bea! Just because we heal quickly doesn't mean that we don't need rest after delivering a pup, or in your case three." She stood next to his sister, who still hadn't broken eye contact, and took her pulse. "You seem fine but maybe we could go back in the room, and I can check on you more thoroughly."

"Kyle?" she asked again. She looked hurt. He couldn't deal with the only family he had hating him. He knew that plenty of people had gone through that and survived but he just didn't know if he had it in him. He tried to speak but all he could do was open and close his mouth like a dying fish. Before he could manage any words Gemma spoke up.

"Instead of grilling your brother, I need you to get back in bed and let me check you out." She put her hand on the small of Bea's back and steered her into the exam room.

Daniel's arms around him tightened. "Are you alright? I didn't think your sister would have a problem with this. I'm sorry."

His apology woke me out of my stupor. "Don't apologize. This is a beautiful gift, a miracle, or blessing, or… whatever. Please don't apologize to me that we were lucky enough to find each other. Especially after just talking me off a ledge." Kyle sighed and tucked himself tighter against Daniel. "I will talk to her. I'm sure it will be fine." He wasn't sure at all.

~

"Well," Gemma started, rolling back from the table, and removing her gloves. "you are doing great. How much would you say the pups have eaten? Do you need help with them? Are they latching on correctly?"

"They're fine. They took turns on the breast and never stopped, even when it ached, I let them keep on, I read the books and stuff. I know all about what I'm doing. Before we left, my best friend was considering going to school to be a doula and lactation specialist. Lots of books were laying around, but we have you now, so I guess that won't be needed. What's going on with you two and my brother? Because let me tell you, Doctor that delivered my pups or not, I will kick your ass. He isn't good with the relationship stuff. It's left him a little insecure and I don't want him to hurt any more than he was when that last woman dumped him. She was cruel to him. Hurt him a lot." Her eyes held concern and love, so Gemma decided to cut her a break, even though her wolf was offended that this person could think she'd betray or intentionally hurt her mate.

"Don't worry. I promise that we have no desire to hurt Kyle. As soon as I walked in last night, I knew Kyle was my mate. Fortunately, all of our wolves calmed down enough for us to get through your labor and delivery before raging back full force and making us… um…."

Bea smiled. "Lose control?"

"Yes?"

"So, you're both here for the long haul, not just messing with him?" Gemma nodded. Making her way to the small pups keeping warm in the incubator. "You put all three in one? They seem to like cuddling and warmth. I agree with you, they should be together. There have been quite a few studies done on multiples healing and growing better and faster when they are put together in one bed." She had one hand in the incubator and was taking the pulse of each pup and seemed to be feeling their little heartbeats with her hand. Being a shifter made things like that easier, no stethoscope needed. "Did you name them yet?" She looked up to Bea.

"Um, yes." She smiled down at her pups. "Meet Tabbie, Kylie, and Jack."

Gemma didn't realize anyone had come into the room until she heard Kyle speak, with a choked-up voice. "They are amazing. You named them after Mom and Dad and me?"

"Of Course. But Tabbie is for mom and for Tabitha." She looked over at where Gemma now stood next to Daniel. "My mom's name was Tabbie. Not short for anything, just a family name. But when Tabitha was born, her mom, my mom's bestie, named her for her friend but made it Tabitha, so there wouldn't be two Tabbies running around the same pack. Tabitha has been my best friend since birth." She looked back to her brother. "You're ok? Having mates?" Gemma thought it seemed like an odd question, unless Bea had already known that her brother was ace and that he struggled with relationships because of that.

"Yes. They know all about me and are still happy to have me as a mate."

The siblings didn't speak for a moment. Finally, Bea broke the silence. "Tabs is my mate." She blurted it out in a quick burst and her face showed her nerves. "We feel like we will have a third but haven't found them yet. I should've told you sooner. I knew you weren't like the bad seeds in the pack, but I was afraid of losing my only family. I don't think I would've survived. It's hard enough being the support for Tabs while she had to move here and none of her family came with her. They all stayed back. We are it for her. Well, us and the pups. All four."

"How did you manage to let someone else touch your mate? And how did she do it?"

"We planned it. We are… synced. So, we went to a shifter friendly bar, we were lucky to find a shifter we didn't know. We had talked about wanting pups but had no desire to wait for ages until we met our mate, if we even really have one. After we met him, we spent a week with him in the city, told him the truth and he said he'd be willing to help. We have his info in case there is ever an emergency, he insisted, and we gave him our info, but he knew that we were mates and that we didn't really want a dad for the pups, just the pups. We figured that when we finally met our mate, they would understand."

Everyone seemed to be absorbing what she had said. This time it was Daniel that broke the awkward silence. "Don't worry about your brother. Both Gemma and I know what a gift it is to find your true mate, we won't take him for granted, or get sick of him, or hurt him. The three of us will make sure we always take care of each other. No matter the need. I promise."

The group all jumped a little when there was a knock at the front door followed by the sound of it slowly opening and a nervous, "Hello?".

The look on Bea's face let them all know who was there and made Gemma wonder if Kyle could have possibly known about her and Tabitha all along and just didn't mention it, because Bea's face told anyone looking that she was in love with the person that just spoke.

"Back here!" Daniel hollered and made his way toward the door to greet the visitor and bring her back. She was right.

"Hi." Tabitha's voice was a little nervous. She looked as if she wanted to fidget but her hands held a large platter of food.

"I finally told my brother. We don't need to hide."

The smile that broke out across Tabitha's face was beautiful and lit up the whole room. "I'm glad. I brought breakfast. I think if we grab some bagels or toast from the kitchen here, then it will stretch enough for all of us." She looked around the room at each of them.

Gemma spoke for them all. "Thank you so much. But honestly, we were about to go into town for our own breakfast." She smiled sweetly, both men smiled too, catching on quickly that Gemma was trying to give these mates alone time after the birth of their pups. "I have checked on all four of them and they are doing great. There is a landline in the kitchen. My cell number is on the fridge. If you have any problems or concerns then please call, but I'm sure we will be back in just a couple of hours." She turned to Bea. "Are you comfortable with me leaving for a couple of hours? Answer honestly, not with your kind nature that wants your brother to have brunch with his mates." She smiled down at Bea who let out a small laugh before answering.

"I feel great. Maybe a little weak, but nothing I'm too concerned about. I might have a shower if that's alright?"

"That's fine as long as you have Tabitha in the room with you. You are still at risk of falling because you used every ounce of your energy last night. Falling would be bad. And even if she's in there with you she will be able to hear the pups if they cry. Just leave both doors open. I'll put a note on the door when we leave, so no one should come in."

Both women nodded at her instructions and smiled. They looked a little nervous, but didn't all first-time parents get a little nervous the first time they were left alone with their little pups?

11

They finished taping a note to the door and were headed towards the cabin Kyle was currently sharing with Bea. Kyle was the only one of them with a car here. In the city Gemma had taken her bike everywhere or called for a rideshare when the weather was too wet for that. And Daniel had come in the helicopter. While technically that was transportation, Gemma doubted there was an airport anywhere in the small town. As they reached the silver Subaru that was probably 20 years old Gemma spoke up. "I had wondered why she had one of the only two-bedroom cabins. I had guessed it was for the triplets. Didn't realize she had a brother living with her. Do you think Tabitha will move in with her now that they've announced their mating?"

Kyle seemed to think about that for a beat. "I hope so. I'm kind of sad she didn't trust me with that information before. Don't tell her I said that."

Gemma smiled and reached for the handle of the back passenger door. Daniel's hand beat her there. "No way," he started "my mother would kill me if I let my mate and really, any woman, sit in the back when I was fully capable of doing it myself."

Gemma smiled and let him lead her to the front seat. "I'll allow it. But just so you know I'm a strong independent woman. I have survived medical school, two speciest packs, and being a female medical resident in a predominantly male hospital. I can survive the back seat. Sometimes I will want to cater to you as well."

Daniel sighed. "OK. But if my mom gets mad at me, I'm blaming you." All three chuckled as they got themselves buckled in.

⁓

The ride to town took a while but they used the time to talk and get to know each other. Unlike the human couples she knew they didn't spend forever on small talk that didn't really matter in the long run. Gemma thought that probably came from knowing that they were fated. Of course, they still had nerves and doubts, Kyle's morning conversation showed them that, but for the most part they felt confident in the fact that they could make this work.

Gemma loved getting to know her mates. Kyle loved Halva, which he could rarely find in their old pack and there was no way he'd find it here, and he hated black licorice, so much so that he warned them that he'd gag and maybe puke if either of them ate it around him. Daniel was afraid of butterflies and moths. They laughed at learning that. He wasn't sure why, but he'd always hated them. His favorite food was bacon wrapped filet with horseradish crust. He spoke of it with an almost creepy reverence. She admitted her love of Science Fiction movies and tv and the men proceeded to quiz her on her knowledge and judge her on the fact her favorite 'Star' franchise was SG-1. That all stopped when it was revealed that Kyle was a Trekkie and Daniel had a collection of lightsabers, including the black one. They were playfully mocking each other and making Gemma laugh for the rest of the drive.

The diner was on Main Street and that street was basically the entire town. It had a few stores up and down each side and then it was nothing but trees as far as you could see, ending in a large, centralized park at the end of the street in front of what seemed to be City Hall. They made their way inside and Gemma was surprised to see it almost filled to capacity. Not that capacity was more than about 50 people. A young girl, probably 16 or 17 walked up to them with a smile. She was wearing a small black apron and a name tag that read 'Beppie' but that was the only indication that she worked there. Looking around Gemma saw that all the employees, all three of them, counting the cook, just wore plain clothes. She liked it. Made her feel like she was visiting a friend instead of sitting in a room full of strangers.

"Morning. Just the three of you?" Her voice was sweet with a sing-song quality.

Daniel spoke for them. "Morning Beppie, yes, just the three of us."

She gave Daniel a big smile that made Gemma want to stake her claim. That was a new feeling for her.

Beppie grabbed a few menus and led them back to a u-shaped booth. Without even discussing it Daniel and

Gemma led Kyle into the booth first so they could sit on either side of him. "Can I get you some juice or coffee while you look at the menu?"

They all requested coffee and she left them to look over the menus.

"They seem to have a theme." Kyle spoke quietly from between them. "The Early Bird Special, The Two Birds One Stone, The Swan Song…"

"That is pretty clever though. It's fun. I bet their lunch menu is the same." Daniel smiled at them.

Beppie returned and took their orders. Two Swan Songs and a Goose with a Golden Egg. They took the time to fix their coffee to their liking before they started talking again. It was Daniel who finally broke the silence.

"I will need to call my parents today, and my brother Elkan, and the rest of my siblings can wait. And we need to figure out the living situation. I think we will all fit in the clinic apartment, as long as we get a better bed, but when do you want to have us move in?" He sighed and rubbed his hand over his face. "Sorry, I'm being presumptuous. I was assuming that's what you wanted but know that might not be the case."

Gemma quickly reached her hand across the table and placed it on top of Daniel's. "I know I'm progressive and independent. That doesn't mean I want to live apart from my mates. I do appreciate you taking the time to see that I might not want that and giving me an option. That is very important to me. I haven't lived in a pack for years and I'm used to the human world."

"OH MY GOSH! I knew it!" They had been so preoccupied that they didn't notice Beppie making her way over with a plate of corn bread. "I told my dad that all the people coming through town seemed like shifters. He thought I was crazy. He still thinks we are the only kind of shifters there are. That is so bizarre, why do older people think that?" She obviously didn't expect an answer because she set the plate down and continued speaking without missing a beat. "What kind of shifters are you? Did your pack move into the abandoned campground? Are you just here for a while or did you move in for good?" Gemma wanted to laugh at her enthusiasm but struggled with her newfound jealousy again as Beppie sat down in the booth next to Daniel.

Daniel didn't seem to notice Gemma's unease with the situation and simply laughed and answered the girl. "Slow down, those are a lot of questions. I wouldn't usually talk about pack with an outsider but considering you're a shifter too I will make an exception. Yes, we moved into the campground, yes, we are staying for good, and we are wolves."

"That is so cool." She leaned her elbow on the table, resting her chin in her hand. "I'm a hawk. I've never met a wolf before. Only an owl and a phoenix. My dad says I made that up, but I didn't. It was at an artist summer camp I got a scholarship to. It was down in Idaho. So much fun. Even horseback riding was fun. It was nice meeting other shifters. I am so glad you guys are here. This town is all shifters. Well, we have a couple of human mates, but mostly shifter."

Apparently, Gemma wasn't the only one suffering from jealousy. Kyle spoke up then. "What kind of places do you have in this town? Anything fun? My mates and I would love something fun to do for date night."

Gemma was relieved when the teen's mannerisms

didn't change. It made her feel as if the girl wasn't trying to flirt, just genuinely excited.

"Are you kidding? On this side of the street there's the ice cream shop and the police station, which is in the back of said ice cream shop, and the hardware store, then us, then a thrift shop. The other side of the street has the post office, the market slash general store, Lupe's hair and nail salon, and the sporting goods store. There used to be a bookstore but when Mr. Skye passed no one had the time or inclination to take it over. So, it's empty now. There is also a volunteer fire department on the block behind us, next to the school. Only one school for all the grades. Even the adult education program is run out of the gym."

"Where do you go for medical and dental and such?" Gemma was curious.

"None of us seem to have dental problems, so when there is the odd emergency, we go down the mountain about another hour to the next town. They have a dentist. And we had a healer, but she hasn't done so well since her mate passed. She and Mr. Skye were mates for about 120 years. She just isn't doing great. We will need a new healer soon. Right now, we only go to her with emergencies. For everything else we go down the mountain."

Gemma shook her head and reached into the small wallet she'd brought with her. She pulled out one of her cards. "Can I use your pen?" Beppie passed it to her. Gemma quickly jotted down the land line on the bottom of the card. "Here," she said, passing Beppie the card, "we are going to eventually have a cell tower, but until then use the land line. I'll have to talk to our… mayor before inviting you to the clinic, but if anyone needs me just call and I'll come. Alright?"

Beppie looked down at the card. "A doctor? That is so awesome. I will let people know. Thank you." There was a ding of a bell. "That'll be your food. I'll be right back." She made her way to the half wall between the dining and kitchen and grabbed the three plates. She returned and set them down with a smile. "Is there anything else you need?" When they all answered she smiled again. "Well. Welcome to Hawk's Landing."

12

Daniel was glad to see that there were other shifters in the area that seemed friendly. Time would tell. He didn't want to place all his hope for this pack on one bubbly teenaged girl. He was keeping his fingers crossed though. He knew this small group didn't have anywhere else to go. Mariam would make sure they weren't homeless, but no one needed the added stress, emotionally or financially. Especially Mariam, she had so much on her plate already.

Gemma broke the silence in the car. "That breakfast sandwich was ridiculously good. I think you guys should try it next time, especially if you like goose. It was divine."

"It smelled fabulous. But I haven't had a lot of goose. Even in wolf form. Turns out both forms are afraid of birds." Kyle gave Daniel an exaggerated stink eye when he laughed. Kyle continued. "It's a little pricey to buy and I can't bring myself to intentionally look for one."

They fell into silence again and all seemed to be thinking about more serious things.

"Do you think the entire town will be as nice as Beppie?" Gemma asked the question Daniel had been thinking. So, he answered honestly.

"I really hope so, but even if they're not as welcoming as she was, we just need them to be accepting. I am hoping we don't have to worry about their alpha getting all territorial. I have never met a hawk shifter, not sure if they're better or worse than us. I think when we get back, we need to go straight to Bryce to tell him about this."

"You don't think we should call Alpha Mariam?" Kyle's question was valid, and Daniel realized that his mate was feeling very anxious. Gemma must've been able to tell as well because she reached over her hand and placed it on the back of his neck, giving a gentle squeeze.

Kyle made eye contact in the mirror and Daniel realized no one had answered his question. "No, I think it's important we still respect the hierarchy of the pack. If he fails to inform her that will be a different conversation, but he needs to have the opportunity to show Mariam that he respects her as his Alpha."

Kyle gave a nod and let out a deep breath. "That makes sense." They turned onto the dirt road that led to the camp. Someone was repainting the sign. Daniel hoped they renamed the camp. The previous name was a made-up word that was supposed to sound Native American. Someone had thought it was acceptable before, but he really hoped this pack realized that it wasn't. Kyle parked his car next to the clinic instead of where they had gotten the car from earlier by Tabitha's cabin.

When they stepped out of the car, they could hear a little cry coming from inside the clinic. Kyle seemed worried but just as before Gemma calmed him down with a hand to his neck. "Don't worry, that's a regular angry cry, not a hurt or stressed cry."

Kyle scrunched his brow. "How can you tell?"

Gemma shrugged nonchalantly. "Practice. I've been a doctor for years and my residency was in OB/GYN. I only decided later to be a GP. I did some surgical rounds too. Not a preference and it doesn't come up too often with our healing, but I wanted to have that experience in case of emergencies."

Daniel walked them to the door and then reached down and took one of their hands in his. "I'm going to go tell Bryce about the shifters. Unless you think he'd take that information better coming from you?" He was looking at Kyle. Kyle simply shrugged then shook his head.

"No, you go. Please."

Daniel was afraid there was a story there, but none of them had the time right now to get into the discussion. He leaned in and gave Kyle a little peck on the lips before tuning to Gemma and giving her the same.

"I'll be back in a few minutes."

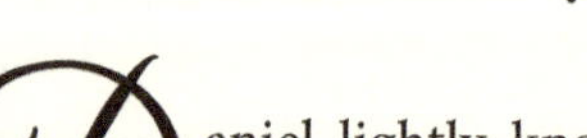

Daniel lightly knocked on the office door that he'd been led to.

"Come on in." Bryce's voice boomed from the other side of the door.

Daniel entered and closed the door behind himself. The room was boring and utilitarian, but Bryce was in the process of hanging some photos on the wall behind the boring beige desk.

"I love these little strips, no more looking for a stud, and if I change my mind, I can simply remove it and start again. They are genius." His smile was genuine.

"My mom will only use those now; she has banned people from pounding nails into all the walls. Claimed we were worse than termites."

"What can I help you with Daniel?" Bryce wasn't being rude, just a straightforward kind of guy.

"We went into town for breakfast. Me and my mates…" Before he could finish Bryce interrupted.

"Mates? When did this happen? And who?"

"Sorry, should've started with that, especially since we are planning on staying here so I'll be moving in, as long as that's alright. I was lucky enough to find my fated mates, Kyle and Gemma."

"Well congratulations. That is amazing. And we will love having you live here. Now I'm just wishing I hadn't already gotten Kyle and Bea settled into that bigger cabin. The other two-bedroom cabins I assigned to mated pairs with children. Dang, I don't want to have to ask her to move after just having her pups."

"Id' hold off on making any decisions about that. Just give Bea a few days to come talk to you." Bryce looked curious but simply nodded. "Real reason I'm here. We went to breakfast in town, Hawk's Landing, and it turns out the entire town is hawk shifters. I'm not sure if there are going to be any issues with that. But Gemma gave the nice waitress a card with the clinic's landline on it, so I'm sure the hawk alpha already knows. We just wanted to make sure you were aware. I don't think there is going to be any problems but wanted to make sure we were all prepared if there is a problem."

"Thank you, I will call Alpha Mariam and let her know. I'm pretty sure she'll want us to stick around and see what happens, but it's her call. Hawks. I only realized there were other kinds of shifters recently. I am looking forward to meeting them. I hope they are feeling the same way."

Daniel gave a smile and a nod, glad that Bryce seemed to be settled into the role of Mayor instead of Alpha well. "Then I will head back over and help Kyle get his things moved into the clinic apartment."

13

Kyle left Gemma to take care of his sister and the pups while he walked over to the cabin to grab his few things. They hadn't had a lot of space in the car when they left, it seemed more important to him that his sister and Tabitha have the things they needed. The three of them had driven his car out. So many bathroom breaks. He didn't want to ask them to get rid of the baby things they'd been collecting since they discovered they'd be having pups. It didn't seem right. So, he managed with a shoe box full of mementos and a duffle bag of clothes. So, making the short trek would suffice, no need to drive over to get his stuff.

He made quick work of putting his clothes back into his duffle and grabbing his favorite mug from the little kitchen table. His sister had made it for him in fourth grade. It was bright green with blobs of yellow that were supposed to be flowers all over it. His name was painted in black with wobbly letters. She gave it to him because it was supposed to be a Father's Day gift for their dad. Their mom and dad had died a couple of years before and they had been staying in Alpha Bryce's house until Kyle was sixteen and able to take care of her. He knew a lot of people hadn't forgiven Bryce for his mistakes yet. He wasn't one of those people. Alpha Bryce took them in then, once he was 16, put them up in the small gardener's cottage that was behind the Alpha house. He and his mate made sure they always had easy food stocked and they never wanted for anything. He was a man that made mistakes, but that didn't make him unforgivable.

He shoved the mug on top of the clothes and zipped up the bag, reaching up and grabbing his small box from the closet shelf tucked in under his arm. Pulling the bag up on his opposite shoulder he made his way out of the little cabin that had been home for less than a week. He really hoped Bea and Tabitha would be happy here.

*K*yle got to the door of the clinic the same time as Daniel. "What did Bryce have to say about the hawk shifters?"

Daniel opened the door for him and ushered him in. "He was mostly curious I think, but he said he was going to call Mariam. I wouldn't be surprised if he's already on the phone with her. I'm glad. I was worried he wouldn't let go of his Alpha role and try to handle it all himself."

Kyle set his things down at the bottom of the stairs and followed Daniel toward the kitchen. He could hear Gemma and Bea talking and one of the pups fussing. "Nah, he's wanted to step away from the role for quite a while. Was trying to find a worthy alpha to take over for him. No one came along and then the others mutinied. I think he was hoping Tom would be up for it even though he was a beta. You know how that turned out."

Daniel grabbed them each a bottle of water out of the fridge and passed it over. "You are one of the few people that has positive feelings and loyalty for Bryce."

Kyle shrugged. "I've known him my entire life. Lived with him after our mom and dad died. I think that a lot of the people you have met feel like he failed them, and maybe he did, but he tried to make it better. Redeem the pack. Redeem himself. Mostly he just wanted to protect everyone he could and if he'd said anything about the behaviors of others in the pack that were destructive, they would've killed him, and it all would've been for nothing. He knew some people ran away. He did his best to make sure that they weren't followed. It was the best he could do."

Daniel tilted his head, as if he was absorbing the words. "I didn't realize you were so close. Didn't know that he had done so much for you. I hope I haven't said anything to offend."

"No. I would've said something. I didn't volunteer the information. I don't expect anyone from outside our pack to know." He smiled at Daniel to let him know that he had no bad feelings.

Daniel smiled back and for a moment it completely distracted him from everything. No one has a right to be that sexy. Before he lost his senses entirely the phone rang, startling both of them. Daniel was closest so he answered.

"Hello."

The voice that answered was somehow gruff and

songlike at the same time. "Hello, I got this card from Beppie."

"Oh hello, yes, my mate gave Beppie her card. Wanted to make sure the hawks had her number in case there was an emergency. Is there something wrong? Do you need me to drive her into town for someone?"

The line was silent for a beat before he answered. "So, you are shifters? Interesting. No, we have no emergency. My name is Jeremy, I'm Alpha. Mate wants me to invite y'all to a picnic at the town square this coming Saturday, 'bout noon. It's potluck, ouch, hmmm, mate says not to worry about it if you can't bring anything, we know you're just getting settled, there should be plenty."

"Thank you, I'll pass the invitation to the rest of the pack, and our Al… leader, Bryce. Can I give him your number in case he has any questions?"

The Alpha rattled off a number. Kyle hung up the phone when he realized Jeremy had already done so.

"Huh." Kyle looked over at Daniel, glad he didn't have to repeat the call to him thanks to shifter hearing.

Daniel shrugged. "Better call Bryce"

"Hello." Bryce's voice was booming and cheerful.

"Hey Bryce, how you doing?" Kyle asked with a smile on his face.

"I'm fine. But I hear congratulations are in order. How are you doing?"

He smiled and looked up to Daniel who shrugged. "I told him."

"I'm doing well. It's a lot, but in a good way."

"I remember that feeling." Bryce chuckled. "So, to what do I owe the pleasure?"

"The hawk's Alpha just called. Invited us all to a picnic

in the town square park this Saturday. Noon, potluck style."

"Thank you, Danny, I will let everyone know. Did they ask us to bring anything else?" Bryce seemed to be taking this seriously and Daniel could sense the excitement in his voice.

"Nope, I asked them that too. They said to just bring ourselves and any potluck we're comfortable with, but even if we couldn't that there would be plenty."

"Perfect. I will let everyone know and figure out rides. Thanks again Danny."

"No problem, let me know if you need anything else."

They disconnected the call just in time for Gemma to come out and announce that she required lunch. The three of them spent time laughing and making sand-wiches together before sitting down to eat.

14

They spent the day cleaning up the clinic and then trying not to laugh while Kyle and Bea argued about the fact that Gemma wanted her and the pups to stay another night. Daniel understood her point. She wanted to spend some alone time with her mate and pups, but he wasn't about to get between siblings fighting or his mate's medical opinion. Daniel stepped outside and sat down on the porch steps. They should get one of those enormous porch swings that lays down into a bed. He was going to put that on the list for the next time he hit up the warehouse store. He took a deep breath and dialed the all too familiar number on the cordless phone from the kitchen. It was time to call mom. He brought the phone up to his ear and waited for the connection.

"Hey baby! Where are you at? You aren't calling to cancel on Sunday dinner, are you?" Her voice was melodic and comforting and brought Daniel peace.

"Unfortunately, I am going to have to cancel. Before

you complain let me explain. I met my mates." He pulled the phone away from his ear to protect his eardrum from her loud whoop.

"Tell me all about them. What pack are they in? When will you be moving them home?"

He sighed knowing she wouldn't like part of this conversation. It was horrible when Adam and Ben had to leave, and then his twin Elkan, she hated to see any of her pups move away. "I'm going to be moving here mom. One of my mates is the new doctor up here in Wyoming. I don't think it should shock us anymore that a lot of our mates are in Hidden Pack. Mariam needs Gemma here."

His mom replied, a lot less excited than she'd been just a moment ago. "I understand. I don't have to like it though. When do you think you will be able to get them here to meet me and your father?"

"I'm not sure. We are still trying to get Gemma set up in the clinic, get Kyle and I moved into the clinic apartment, and now we have an odd situation regarding hawk shifters."

"Hawk shifters?!" He pulled the phone away from his ear again. "I have never met another species of shifter. That is amazing."

"I thought so too. The closest town is Hawk's Landing, aptly named as it turns out. The entire town is hawk shifters, except for a few human mates. Tomorrow we are having a potluck picnic lunch in the town square. Hopefully it goes well. We went to the diner in town this morning for breakfast and met a lovely girl named Beppie, who couldn't have been more than 17, she was the one who told us they were shifters and when we left, she took the info to her Alpha, which was the right thing to do."

"Beppie?" His mom's voice sounded odd, like the tone she'd get when she was searching for her keys or the misplaced grocery list.

"I'm not sure what it's short for."

"I'm going to have to check but I think that Beppie is an old family name in both your father's family and mine. We actually considered naming Bess that but decided we didn't want to use the abbreviated name as her name. I think Beppie is short for Elizabeth."

Daniel shrugged. "Huh. That's odd. I'll have to ask her when I see her tomorrow." He looked up to see one of the young boys from the pack running over.

"Mr. Daniel, Mr. Bryce wants to know if you have something planned to bring tomorrow or if he should make a sausage casserole for y'all to bring."

Pulling the bottom of the phone away from his mouth he spoke. "We're ok, Kyle is inside whipping something up. Tell him I said thank you though.

He smiled as the boy ran back the way he'd come from. He heard his mom laughing on the other end of the line. "What's so funny?"

"Just laughing at the normalcy which your life has entered."

"Are you saying that I'm boring?" He mocked gasped.

They spent a few more minutes talking, with him promising to come visit as soon as possible and that he would let her know if they needed anything for the clinic or the loft before they said goodbye and hung up.

"She sounds nice." Kyle's voice behind him sounded a little nostalgic.

"She is. Ridiculously nice. And I hope you know that you, Gemma and even your sister, Tabitha and the pups are considered family now. I didn't even tell her that your parents had passed, and she considers you a son already, that's just how she is."

Kyle sat on the step next to him and leaned his head on Daniel's shoulder.

Daniel didn't speak for a while but finally broke the silence while sliding his arm around Kyle's shoulders. "I need you to take the lead with our affection. I've never had an asexual lover; I don't want you to ever feel like you must be physical with us even if you don't want to. Your feelings are important. I want to touch you all the time, but I'm not sure yet when that is welcome."

Kyle shrugged his shoulders and answered. "I love touch. I crave it, especially with you and Gemma, I just might not want to have actual sex. I did yesterday, I wanted it badly, which is confusing me. Maybe I'm more demi than ace? But don't ever be afraid to touch me. I love it."

"What about kissing and such?"

"That's more complicated. I like the romance of making out and cuddling, but I don't necessarily need it to go further than that."

Daniel took that information for a moment, ruminated on it. Finally, he decided to go with his gut. He reached over his other hand and lightly lifted Kyles's chin, bringing his lips up high enough that he could reach down and give him a small kiss. The kiss quickly deepened and grew more passionate, while remaining intimate and soft.

"You guys are beautiful. I am never going to get sick of

seeing you together. Even before the kiss, just the sight of you guys cuddling was exhilarating." They both jumped a little at Gemma's voice. She chuckled. "I didn't mean to make you stop or startle you."

Daniel smiled up at her where she stood leaning on the front door frame. "You liked surprising us, you're a horrible liar. It's not often you get to startle a shifter."

She shrugged but didn't deny it. "And to give a little insight to what you were talking about earlier. From what I understand, the longer we are mated the more we will be attuned with each other's emotions and desires and needs. We won't have to guess when one of us needs something because we will feel it."

Daniel nodded his head, agreeing with her. "I should've thought of that. My brother is so connected with his mates that they share dreams. My other brother can hear his mate when they are in wolf form. My sisters have all sorts of freaky-deaky powers with their mates. I don't know why that didn't occur to me."

Kyle spoke from where he leaned on Daniel's chest, he was slowly sinking, he was probably tired. "When it's about you it's harder to see the obvious. That has been the case for all time and always will be. It's so much easier to see and explain things for other people than it is for yourself."

The last few words were slurred. His mate was falling asleep.

"Let's get you to bed." He looked up at Gemma who turned to hold the door open. His mate was snoring lightly and more relaxed than he'd ever seen him. Instead of trying to wake him up, Daniel simply reached around and adjusted his hold on Kyle before slowly rising with the man in his arms. He was grateful for his shifter strength. He'd never be able to hold the man like this if he'd been human, let alone walk him up the stairs to the bed.

Daniel carefully put Kyle on the bed before he started removing his shoes and getting him undressed. Gemma helped, quietly removing his button up flannel. The two of them made sure Kyle was comfortable before they slowly removed their own clothes and crawled into bed on either side of him. They put their arms around him and closed their eyes. It had been a very eventful few days and it had caught up with them all.

⁓

*D*aniel woke to the sight of Gemma and Kyle slowly kissing and loving each other next to him. He enjoyed watching his mates learn each other's bodies. Their likes and dislikes. He was especially interested to learn what Kyle did and didn't like. What he did or didn't need. He wanted to make sure and absorb as much information about that as possible. Daniel could admit he was worried about offending his mate. It was the last thing he wanted to do. His job was to protect his mates. Physically, emotionally, in every regard. He was afraid he would mess up and hurt the feelings of someone he was already half in love with.

After watching them for what seemed like forever, he just couldn't stop himself from touching them. He reached out his hand and slowly rubbed it down Kyle's back, from nape and over his beautiful ass. Two sets of eyes looked over at him. Gemma smiled. "Did you want some love too? We just wanted a little cuddle time before we have to get ready."

Before Daniel could answer Kyle interrupted. "I need to get in the shower. I promised to move Tabitha's things over to Bea's cabin before we left for the picnic." He gave a last loud kiss to Gemma and rolled himself off the bed. Both Gemma and Daniel watched him walk away and into the bathroom.

"Go join him. I just can tell he's still feeling insecure. Don't let him." Gemma looked at him, practically begging him with her eyes.

He leaned over and gave her a kiss. "Of course not. I'll go wash his back."

Gemma grabbed his hand as he was getting out of the bed. "We don't have to know how all of this works. We just have to be willing to work with each other without censure. We can do that right?"

Daniel gave her hand a squeeze. "I will never hurt or judge either of you intentionally. My only goal now is to make sure that the rest of your lives are as full of joy and love and happiness as is possible. You two are my world."

Gemma gave him a smile before pulling her hand back and using it to make a 'move along' motion toward the bathroom. Daniel smiled and set out to join his mate in the shower.

Kyle was looking towards the door when Daniel walked in, making eye contact through the foggy glass of the shower doors. From the look in his eyes, Daniel figured he'd overheard their conversation in the bedroom. Daniel gave him a smile and made his way to the sink.

The fresh smell of toothpaste in the air made him aware of his morning breath. "I'm going to brush my teeth really quick, and some other stuff, but then I'd love to shower with you."

Kyle gave him a self-conscious smile and nodded.

Daniel finished up the necessary business and slid the glass door open to join his mate who was still facing away from him. He reached forward and wrapped his arms around Kyle, resting his head on the nape of his neck. He didn't do anything else or ask for anything, just hugged his mate close and hoped his love shone through somehow.

After a few long minutes Daniel could feel the tension to start to leave Kyle's body. When he could tell that Kyle was back to himself, he reached one hand over to the little hook where a bright green bath puff hung and grabbed it. He made quick work of soaping it up. He took a small step back and started cleaning Kyle. He began at his neck and thoroughly and slowly worked his way down. When he got to Kyle's ass, he could feel Kyle start to tense but since Kyle hadn't stopped him, he continued carefully. He washed the beautiful globes and efficiently wiped the puff between them. Kyle's breath caught but Daniel didn't think it was because he was excited in any way, just shocked that somebody would wash him so intimately.

Daniel continued down his body and then reached forward and laid a small kiss on his shoulder. "Turn around."

Kyle seemed nervous but did what was asked of him. Daniel repeated the process, starting at his shoulders and making his way slowly down his chest. He could feel Kyle getting more and more nervous the longer it took.

"I don't expect anything. I will not be offended or hurt by your reactions or lack thereof. I just want to do this with you, show you my feelings by washing and tending you."

"But," Kyle started. "you're, ya know, um, hard."

Daniel chuckled. "Yes. You are beautiful and my mate and you're allowing me to touch your body. I'm going to get hard. I know not to force myself onto you. I'm a grown man and can control myself. Even if I can't get this thing under control, I'm not too ashamed to admit that I can handle this all by myself in the shower, and most mornings do. I don't expect anything. Ever. Even if you wanted to try and told me to stop at the last minute, or even balls deep, I would stop." He smiled and leaned in to place a soft kiss on Kyle's lips before getting back to washing his mate. Daniel washed down his stomach and then lightly rubbed the puff over his cock. It seemed to be mildly interested in what he was doing but Kyle's eyes showed his mate's emotional desires didn't have the same needs, so he quickly moved on to the muscled thighs and legs.

When he was done, he hung the poof back up and gave Kyle another sweet kiss. "Thank you for letting me take care of you. Both my wolf and I found it very satisfying."

Kyle looked up into his eyes and seemed to be looking for something. He finally spoke, with genuine surprise in his voice. "You mean that, don't you?"

Daniel gave a slight nod and responded. "Of course. I will never lie to you. OK, let me clarify, I might lie about silly things like 'did you enjoy that experimental recipe I tried?' or 'am I still sexy with a bowl cut?' but my father assured me that those don't count."

Kyle started laughing, resting his forehead against Daniel's chest. He laughed for a bit before looking back up into Daniel's eyes. "I never thought I would find someone that truly liked taking care of me. And I would love to do the same for you."

"Not a chance." Gemma's voice made them both jump. "You two can get all cuddly later, we are going to be late and I hate being late."

"Yes dear." Daniel had a laugh in his voice when he answered.

They finished up the necessary things in the shower and hopped out just in time for Gemma to slip in behind them and start getting herself ready.

The three were quickly finished and made their way downstairs to grab their potluck contribution and take off. Tabitha was waiting downstairs and talking to Bea. "Go. Keep my brother company, you know he hates these things."

Tabitha was going to argue but before she could Bea spoke again. "Please. You need the fresh air, and I need sleep. They are all fed and clean and just fell asleep. It's time for me to nap with them. You'll probably be back before they're even awake."

Kyle made his way to the two young women, and Daniel could hear him talking to them both. Making sure everyone would be happy. Daniel was starting to think that was Kyle's natural response to life, making sure everyone was happy. He looked over towards Gemma, they seemed to be thinking the same thing, that they would need to make sure that they always took care to keep Kyle happy and cared for. Maybe their mate link was starting, he swore he could hear or feel what Gemma had been thinking.

Kyle walked out with Tabitha on his arm. "We are ready to go, I promised to keep a close eye on Tabs and that I'd keep my phone on just in case Bea needs me. I put the cordless next to her bed."

"Sounds good."

15

aniel sat in the front. Next to Kyle, on the way into town. They had silently agreed that Tabitha would most likely be more comfortable with Gemma in the back seat. The drive was uneventful. But Tabitha seemed to be enjoying her surroundings.

"I fell asleep on the way here. Didn't wake up until we pulled up in front of the cabin. Seeing all of this. Is amazing., really is a very beautiful place."

They talked about the weather and some other pleasantries as they passed on the way into town. As soon as they drove down Main Street, they could see cars parked all around the town square at the end of the road. They saw many cars from their own pack, as well as many they didn't recognize. They parked and both Daniel and Kyle hopped out to help. Daniel grabbing the casserole dish Gemma had held and Kyle making sure that Tabitha didn't strain too much getting out of the car.

They could see plenty of people from the pack already sitting. Unfortunately, it didn't look like the two packs were mingling very much. From his right Daniel could see Beppie coming toward them with another girl that looked so much like her it had to be a sister. "Thank gods you're here. Help. No one is talking and it's getting mega awkward. This is my sister Mena, b-t-dubs. Help. Make them play nice." Daniel wasn't sure why they had become the masters of mingling, but he gave her a smile anyways.

"I'll see what I can do, promise. This is my sister-in-law Tabitha, her mate had to stay home, she had triplets less than 72 hours ago. So, my better third told her she had to stay back and rest."

Both Beppie and Mena smiled and then spent some time oohing and ahhing over the belly. When it seemed they were done with the introductory chit chat Daniel spoke. "So, show me your Alpha, your healer, and the most influential old person, and I know you know who I mean."

Beppie laughed. "Our Alpha is at the far table wearing a blue flannel shirt and ugly as sin khaki cargo pants. His wife has an awful flower sweater from the 80's. Our healer is sitting at the next table over. She is the one that looks like she should still be living in 1969, with the silver dreads and about 100 yards of material in her crazy dress. And there are in fact two old gossiping men that have everyone in the pack's ears, their wives do too, the four of them are way back by the oak tree playing mahjong. You can't miss them."

"Perfect. I will see what I can do. Can you guys take Tabitha and introduce her around?" He turned his head towards Kyle "Do you want to go with them, or do you want to tackle winning over the old people?"

"Ew, no, I don't want to be in charge of anything that

important. I'll stay with Tabs." The look of fear on Kyle's face was almost comical.

The four of them walked towards the large tables laden with food. Daniel looked over at Gemma. "Alright. Let's grab Alpha Bryce who is hiding in the car that pulled up right after us. We will introduce him to the Alpha Hawk, then introduce you to the healer, then I'll go and try to win over the elders. Sounds like a plan?" She didn't answer right away so Daniel was getting a little nervous. Had he overstepped?

"You're good at this. I can tell you are a natural leader. Is your entire family like this?" She had a big smile on her face.

"Um. I think I forgot to tell you something important. My last name. Redfoot. My dad and uncle are two of the Elders on the Council. My mom is an Alpha and a Doctor. And a vet, technically." He blushed. "So ya, we're all like this."

Gemma shrugged. "Impressive pedigree. You look like you thought I was going to get upset. Just because I don't feel like I belong in a pack doesn't mean I'm anti pack or council. Don't worry, I'm not upset." She leaned over and gave Daniel a smacking loud kiss right on the lips. "Let's save Bryce, his wife is about to kill him if he doesn't get out of the car."

The two of them made their way over to the older sedan that the Alpha was currently hiding in. Not that Daniel would say that out loud.

Apparently just seeing them head over made the Alpha finally decide to get out of the car. By the time they got there the Alpha and his mate were grabbing some containers from the back seat.

Daniel spoke up. "What can I carry?" Before long he and Gemma had full arms of side dishes and salads. "Let me take you over to meet the hawk Alpha, that is our best course of action I think." Bryce nodded his head and the four of them walked toward the Alpha and his mate.

Daniel wasn't so sure why Bryce was so nervous. He'd been to plenty of multi pack meetings from what Daniel understood, so why was this one different. As soon as the introduction was out of his mouth he understood. "Hello Alpha, I'm Daniel. I was the one that met Beppie at the diner, and this is Al…um … Bryce. Our mayor?"

The hawk Alpha looked confused, so Bryce tried to explain. "I'm a retired Alpha. We are part of a much larger pack that is mostly spread out, our little group here still wanted to live regular pack life, so our Alpha Mariam asked me to take up the role of leader, not Alpha though, I know, it's odd."

For a moment Daniel was worried that the hawk Alpha was going to react badly, then he started chuckling. "Retired? I didn't know that was an option. I'm sitting here waiting for one of these young kids to challenge me. Now I'm wondering if there is a better way. Have a seat Bryce, and I'm assuming this is your mate?"

Daniel and Gemma waved them off and dropped off the food at the tables before heading over to the Healer. As soon as they grew near the woman Daniel liked her even more. Her silver dreads were pulled up in a big bun balanced magically on the top of her head. Her nose was pierced, her ears were gauged and smelled exactly like purple kush.

Gemma took the lead here. "Hello, I wanted to introduce myself. I'm Dr Gemma, we just opened up a clinic in the campground." The huge smile she gave Gemma was encouraging.

"Goddess bless. I have been sending out prayers, or thoughts, or meditation, or whatever the fuck you want to call it, into the universe. I am nearly on my deathbed. I have been hoping for another healer, or in this case an actual doctor. I'm so excited to get to know you better." The woman had a raspy voice that you'd love to hear on the radio.

Gemma laughed. "I'm glad to be here. But let's be honest, you're only a little older than I am." A look crossed Gemma's face. "Wait, I have no idea of the natural lifespan of hawk shifters." And just like that the two women were off and discussing things that were flying over Daniel's head.

"Ladies, I am going to step away, enjoy." He gave Gemma a kiss on her cheek and nodded at the Healer. "See you in a bit."

Daniel walked over to the four elders sitting under the oak. Yes, they had their mahjong tiles lined up, but he could tell they were more focused on the people talking and mingling. They were nosy old folks, his specialty.

"Good afternoon, my name is Daniel, part of the pack that just moved into the old campground. I thought you might like some buckeyes before the pups, uh... kids, got ahold of them. I'd love to take credit, but honestly, my mate Kyle made them." He held out the small plate for them. "Sorry, didn't mean to offend. We call our young pups, what do you call the young hawks?"

One of the men grabbed a buckeye and popped it in his mouth. "Never had a buckeye. Like a peanut butter treat. I like it." He grabbed a second one. "We used to call them eyas back when we were young, but nowadays everyone just says 'kids', apparently eyas was too anti-quated a term for them so people stopped. I think they were just trying to fit in with the humans, but what do I know?"

Daniel knelt by the table, so he was closer to eye level, he didn't want anyone to think he was looking down on them, figuratively or literally. "I really want to know more of the history of the hawks. It has only been recently that we even realized there were different types of shifters."

"We were just talking about that," The woman on his left started. "we have always suspected but it was never confirmed. Our history teaches us that there were, that's the important word there, *were* multiple kinds of shifters. That we banded together to fight off a shared enemy, but even with all that strength and power we lost. They won."

Daniel cocked his head to the side. "Who do you think our enemy was?"

The other woman answered. "We have no idea. They were never named in any of the stories, oral or written, all it said was they seemed to be made of light and that they may even have had the ability to glow. Now we've all speculated, for a while I thought maybe it was a phoenix or something like that, but a few years ago we found an old book when my cousin passed, and the old book listed the phoenix' clans as one of the groups of shifters that helped to fight off the enemy, so I guess it wasn't phoenix'."

"If it is alright with you, and of course your Alpha, I would love to get my brother-in-law out here to look at some of those books and even document the oral stories you have. He recently accepted a posting with the Wolf

Council to modernize all of our collected books, some of which are hundreds of years old. If not older. He found some mention of that same war you speak of. So maybe between the wolf books and the hawk books we can get some better information. Of course, if you want to participate in sharing your information we would obviously do the same."

The man that hadn't spoken yet finally broke his silence. "We don't have a council in that same sense. We have a historian in every kettle, as well as an elder that stays in his kettle but meets with the other elders once a month. The historians do too. The Alphas, historians, healers, and elders only meet once a year. That would be me, the elder. Fortunately, we don't have to travel to meet now, our next Zoom is tomorrow. I will bring it up with them. The Alpha of our kettle would give his permission as a formality, the real permission has to come from the elders. I don't think it will be a problem." He looked over at the last woman who had spoken. "Gladys, do you think you can bring this up at the historian meeting tomorrow? You guys will want to weigh in too, I'd suspect."

She nodded and grabbed a buckeye for herself. "No problem. I will make sure they know all the details." She looked over to Daniel. "Do you have a card with the elder council information or that of your historian? In case we have questions?"

Daniel flinched. "I didn't bring it with me. Oh, hold on." He set down the plate of buckeyes and grabbed his wallet from his back pocket. "Does anyone have a pen I can use?" Gladys dug one out of her pocketbook and handed it over. "This is my card, I'm adding the clinic landline at the bottom here, until we get the cell tower working it's the only reliable number for me. On the back I'm giving you my dad's name and number, he's on the elder's council, and my brother in law's name and number. He is very young, so if you call him try to be extra nice, he's only been doing this a couple weeks, and is feeling overwhelmed. Doesn't help that he's constantly distracted by my sister, they're waiting until they both turn 18 to fully mate. For now, they are carefully dating under my mom's watchful eye. So, ya, he's doing his best." He passed the card to the man that said he was the elder.

"Thank you, my name is Chuck. This is my brother Will. And these are our mates Gladys and Glenda."

Daniel gave his best smile. "It was great to meet you all. I hope we get to know each other so much better."

~

The wolf pack and the hawk kettle, which was a new word to Daniel, were getting on great. People were chatting, many people had come and introduced themselves to Gemma specifically. Somehow, they had all already learned that she had a clinic and a real medical degree. Between all of that Tabitha had convinced Gemma to train her because she wanted to be a doula or maybe even a nurse. A quick talk with Bryce and a phone call to Mariam and they all agreed that the hawks could come to the campground for medical appointments. In addition, Joey's contact information was shared with the hawks so that they had someone in the know to talk to and get therapy from. It was a very productive afternoon.

It was nearing sundown, they had been here for a few hours and Daniel was pleased it was doing so well, but he was ready to go home. And Tabitha was more than ready to get home. "We told Bea we'd only be a couple hours. It's been almost 5. I'm done. My feet are swollen, and I want my mate. Can we go?"

Kyle was about to give her a snarky remark when he stopped and squinted. "Is there a person hiding in that tree over there?" He indicated a tree that was across the street in front of the police station. Everyone at the table turned to look. Maybe he was going to jump down right then anyhow, or maybe having four sets of eyes turn to stare had startled him. Either way the man suddenly jumped to the ground almost silently and started racing towards their table. More alarming were the five other men that came running towards the park from all different directions. He could barely hear their feet touching on the ground while they ran. He could smell their anger and determination in the air and wondered how he'd missed the scent of danger before now. How did a group of shifters this large not notice half a dozen men spying on them?

He was fast and determined. That first man they noticed ran straight for them and shifted just his hand into long dark claws, they didn't look like those of a wolf, more like a cat like, like a leopard or lion. Daniel wasn't sure what kind of animal shifter he was, but he knew he had to protect the person that the shifter had his eyes on. Tabitha. The man wasn't a blathering beastly mess so he knew it wasn't the same condition that Tom's mate had, the one he'd detected back home that had tried to attack his sister too. This was something else.

All chatter came to an immediate halt. It looked like a well-oiled machine, some of the adults rounding up and huddling around the children. Wolves and hawks together protecting the young. The rest stood and took a fighting stance. These strangers weren't going to hurt their pack, or kettle, or whatever.

The fight was over fast. Faster than he expected. They were strong and formidable and got some good licks in, but the strangers were taken down quickly. Daniel stuck down the first they shifter they saw. The one charging towards Tabitha. Without a second thought he stood in the man's path, He squatted low and used his shoulder and the other shifters momentum to flip the man onto the ground. Before he could recover Daniel had snapped his neck. The sound of a person's life ending was so simple, like a twig breaking or a pencil being snapped in half. Shouldn't it have sounded more... permanent or authoritative? One enemy still breathed. Or wheezed more accurately. "You...cannot...win. You... cannot... mix... the lines..." he looked at Tabitha. "we...will stop... you. The others... will eliminate... the mixed...pups." He turned his head toward their camp. "My brothers... will... finish. Shifters need... to stay... pure. Hawks, Wolves... not... friends...it's wrong." He let out a last rattling breath and faded.

Kyle was up in a heartbeat. Next to him stood Bryce and the hawk Alpha. "We have to get to Bea and the pups. He said there were others." He turned scared eyes to Daniel. "What if we're too late?"

"Let's get in the car and go." Gemma reached to help Tabitha get up and they started towards the car.

"That's going to take too long. I'll shift. Meet you at home." Before anyone could argue he was shifted, his clothes in a shredded pile at their feet.

"Wait!" Daniel shouted at Kyle, who was definitely not waiting, he was already across the town square and headed towards camp. "Shit, hurry and get there Gemma, I'm following Kyle." He quickly shifted, barely listening as he heard Bryce and the Alpha agree to shift and run as well. Or fly. The hawk Alpha called over a couple of his guards to shift and follow too. One looked like a much younger version of the alpha, must be his son, and the other was a woman that looked like she was a fairy tale princess, but Daniel saw the look in her eyes. If she was a princess, then she didn't need anyone to save her.

Bryce and Daniel ran as fast as they could. Trying their best to catch up with Kyle before he got himself into trouble. Above them flew three hawks. Suddenly a howl sounded. Distressed. Bea. Another howl responded and Kyle was still way too far ahead of them. Shit. It was as if the hawks understood the urgency, they no longer waited for the wolves but put on speed and were quickly out of their line of sight. It felt like it took forever to get to the campground. When they broke through the tree line, they saw Kyle and the three hawks fighting off four strangers. The hawks had left their hands shifted and were fighting with talons. Coming up from behind, Daniel didn't even shift back, simply leapt and landed one the back of the stranger closest to Kyle. He ripped out his throat and turned to the others. But there was no one else to fight. The four men all lay dead on the grass and gravel.

Daniel looked over to Kyle in time to see him stagger. He had a huge gash across his chest. He'd lost so much blood. He shifted just in time to catch Kyle as he fell. "Kyle, wake up. Right now. Kyle." He could hear Kyle's

Subaru coming up the drive at a much faster speed than would be considered safe.

"Bea, it's me Bryce, I'm coming in sweetheart." Bryce took a step onto the porch but before he could even turn the handle, they could hear the growls from inside. Bryce turned to Daniel. "I don't know what to do. If she's this upset only her mate can calm her. Do you know where the pup's father is?"

Daniel let out a mirthless chuckle. "No clue, but her mate is just pulling up."

Tabitha was out of the car and running, hands wrapped under her swollen belly, before the car even came to a full stop. "Bea, it's me, I'm coming in." This time the sound was more of a whine. "I'm opening the door now, there are new friends out here you haven't met yet, don't attack them. I promise the bad guys are down." She opened the door, inside was Bea, in wolf form, snarling and walking back and forth protectively around the hallway to the exam rooms. "It's ok. The bad guys are dead. Shift back. I want to check on you and our pups. Please." It took a little longer than normal, but that was common when adrenaline was high. Finally, she looked up at Tabitha from where she was kneeling on the floor.

"He wanted to kill our pups. I don't understand, why would he want to kill our pups?" She had tears in her eyes. "I kept them safe, I promise, I kept our little pups safe." She fully broke down into tears.

Daniel picked up Kyle and looked back to the car and Gemma. "He's hurt, I'm taking him to the other exam room." Gemma was quick on his heels.

Gemma stopped at Bea to take her pulse and look in

her eyes, to make sure she wasn't going into shock. "Where are the pups? In the little bed?"

Bea shook her head. "I didn't know what to do. I hid them under the kitchen sink." Saying it out loud must've broken a little of the stupor that Bea was under. Her and Tabitha hopped up and ran into the kitchen. They quickly opened the cupboard door and reached down to grab the three little swaddled treasures.

Gemma left the couple to care for their pups and hurried into the exam room to care for her own mate. Daniel was clearly upset but his hands stroked gently over Kyle's hair and cheek. "He looks so pale."

Professional Gemma was back. "He's lost blood. Help me take his shirt off and then we will clean his wound and stitch it. If we need to give him blood, which is rare for us, his sister is the same type. But I'll hook up a saline IV and honestly that should be sufficient." Gemma was aware she was rambling, but it helped to keep her focused instead of scared. "Alright hand me some saline and a box of four-inch gauze pads." She snapped on her nitrile gloves and looked up to see Daniel looking around the room confused. Before she needed to explain everything to him again Tabitha walked in.

"I was snooping earlier. I know where it all is." In a matter of seconds, the medical tray held everything Gemma would need for cleaning and suturing the wounds across Kyle's chest. "I'm going to start a saline IV."

Gemma left her to do that and instead focused her attention on cleaning the wound. It was all pretty standard for a shifter fight. Someone had slashed their claws across Kyle's chest. In the wound track she found a piece of whatever claw had been used broken off inside of it.

She carefully removed it and stored it on the tray to inspect later. She finished cleaning the wound and began stitching it up with the dissolving sutures. "Daniel you might have to hold him down, he's starting to wake up and I'm not done yet. The Lidocaine is probably already wearing off too." They were lucky. While he stirred and whined, he didn't fully wake up until Gemma was taping down the last of the gauze.

Kyle slowly blinked his eyes open and looked around the room. Then it was as if all the memories of how he got into this predicament came flooding back. "Where's Bea? The pups?" He tried to sit up.

Daniel kept him down. "Don't try to get up. They're safe, they're all safe. Do you really think Tabitha would be in here, helping us, if her mate was still in danger?"

Kyle looked over at Tabitha who gave him a nod. He laid his head back down. "Ok. Ya. Ok."

He looked immediately drained. He closed his eyes and sighed. "I was so scared. They were headed to the clinic when I got here. They were coming from Bea's cabin. They must have been looking for her specifically. I'm so glad she wasn't where her scent was the strongest." He opened his eyes and looked at Tabitha. "You guys will probably have a mess to clean up in the cabin. Sorry."

Tabitha smacked his leg. "Don't you dare apologize. I was too far away and the size of a barn. I couldn't take care of my mate and you did. So don't you dare apologize." She covered her face with her hands and let out a small hiccuping sob. "I was so scared."

Soon the sound of Bea pushing the little baby bed into the room met their ears. "I was scared too." She didn't have tears in her eyes, but Daniel could tell it was a struggle to not cry. "I wanted to show you that we are all just fine. You protected us again brother. Just like always."

Gemma sighed. "I'll be right back." She headed out to the yard where many more people had arrived. When she stepped out, she saw how nervous everyone was. She looked over to find Bryce and the hawk Alpha still talking in muted voices. "Alpha, Bryce, can I interrupt for a moment?"

Bryce held out his arm and she walked into his embrace. Sure, she didn't need a pack, but she had missed the comfort that an alpha's touch could give you. "Is everyone all right Gemma? I didn't want to walk in and get in the way."

She smiled. "Yes. Everyone is fine. Kyle will be in pain for a day or so, but he's going to be right as rain. The reason I wanted to talk to you. I want blood, tissue, hair, and whatever else I can think of from these people. And I was hoping you could call down to the healer and have her do the same with the ones in town square. We were just attacked by some sort of mystical shifter army, and I want more information."

"This is why you're so trusted by Mariam. And now me too. That is smart thinking. I wouldn't have even thought of that" He turned to look at the hawk Alpha. "Is that alright with you?"

The hawk nodded and asked to use a landline. Gemma led him into the clinic and showed him the phone. She made her way back and saw Bea cuddled on the small bed with Kyle. Tabitha stood on one side with the pups next to her, Daniel on the other rubbing his hands up and down Kyle's arm. Daniel was more stressed out than he'd admit.

The Alpha gave a casual cough to get Gemma's attention and she turned. "Phyllis said she'd get all the things you need. Chuck has already used the plastic zip bags we had at the park to label each of their personal belongings. Phyllis said she'd use his same descriptions so we would know who was who. And Beppie took pics on her phone, said something about identifying marks and not disturbing the scene. I don't follow half of what that girl says. Phyllis will drive up with everything in an hour or so. I think she also wants to check out this fancy new clinic."

Gemma smiled. "Perfect. I will look forward to that. I'm going to make sure I don't have anything else I need to do before they get here." She turned her head and looked in the room at her mates. "Daniel," she waited for him to turn and make eye contact. "after I have everything I need from town I might need you to fly it over to Mariam. Unless she wants me to continue the work from here. But I wanted you to know that you might need to make a quick run back to Oregon tonight."

He nodded his head but still looked shocky. Nope, she was not going to let him fly tonight. The fridge they have here would have to do, until at least tomorrow.

16

The next morning came quickly. Gemma hadn't had a chance to sleep yet. She had spent the evening going over all the blood and tissue samples she'd recovered from the bodies here at camp. She had done full autopsies on each man trying to get as much information about them that might help the pack figure out more about this strange group of men. The men were old, much older than they looked, and Gemma wasn't sure why or how. That fact was driving her crazy. The men had all shared an elk for their last meal, fresh kill, probably in shifted form. Ew, she hoped it was in shifted form. Raw elk would be disgusting. In addition to that she'd noticed a tattoo on the chest of each of the men. It was symbols she'd never seen before. She was going to have to do some research to figure out the meaning behind it.

She reached for her cup of coffee; she was heartbroken to find it empty. She stood from her desk, stretching tall and getting the kinks out of her back. At the last minute she decided maybe she needed a short nap more than another cup of coffee. Gemma walked into the bedroom where Daniel was carefully lying next to Kyle. Kyle had cuddled in and was resting his head on Daniels's chest. His chest was nearly completely healed and looked like nothing more than an angry scar now. Gemma waited for jealousy to hit but instead she was just happy. Happy that her mates were finding comfort with each other. Happy that they were safe. Happy that they were both hers. And she was theirs.

She quietly walked to the bed, trying to not wake up either of the men, and only half succeeding. Daniel cracked his eyes open and gave Gemma a lazy smile. He didn't speak, just used his arm to pull Kyle a little more towards the center of the bed so there was some room for Gemma to rest with them. She crawled in and smiled at Daniel. "I just need to rest my eyes for a minute."

~

"Gemma. Wake up sweetie. Beppie is here with all the photos and the other bodies." She could hear Daniel but had no desire to open her eyes. "Come on. I'll make you a Cafecito."

"Fine. But make it a double."

Gemma drug herself out of bed and made her way to the restroom to splash some water on her face and do the necessary things before she went downstairs to deal with the day. Looking at her watch she calculated that she'd only managed about three hours of sleep. Today was going to suck.

When she walked into the kitchen Beppie was already sitting at the breakfast bar drinking what looked like hot chocolate. "Morning Beppie. How are you holding up?" The kitchen smelled very strongly of cinnamon rolls and coffee. Almost like her mates had purposefully filled the house with pleasant smells. Probably to cover up the smells of what she was doing all night.

Beppie still looked more than a little upset. "I will be fine. I'm still processing I guess." She shrugged. "Something kept bugging me. The men all had these weird tattoos. I couldn't really place it, but they seemed familiar. Phyllis said they look like a combination of multiple Norse runes. She wasn't sure what they meant, it's not like her specialty or anything, she just dated a woman once that was super into stuff like that. So maybe if you know someone that knows about that stuff it could help."

Gemma accepted the cup of delicious brew from Daniel with a smile and sat next to Beppie. "I'll ask around the pack, I'm sure we have someone. If not here at the camp, then someone else in the Hidden Pack."

Beppie seemed to not want to talk about the deaths any longer, so she changed the subject. "So, what is the deal with this pack? I know it's probably rude to ask, but it's super weird that Bryce is like a mayor and not an Alpha. Like, I know he's an alpha, but not the Alpha. Ya know? And where did the name 'Hidden Pack' come from?"

Gemma smiled and took a sip of her coffee. "Well, Bryce was the Alpha of the pack but there was a bit of a difference of opinion and instead of fighting to the death for a pack that was over 50% racist, sexist, and bigoted, he decided to leave. His mate's family owned this campground, so it seemed like a good place to come. The campground was never deeded to the pack. Always stayed in the Alpha mate's name. The people from the pack that were in the same progressive mindset as Bryce came along with him. The Hidden Pack has an Alpha. Mariam. She is the Alpha by a democratic vote. The pack is a ragtag group of people that had to escape or run away or just disappear for whatever reasons and they managed to find Mariam through one way or another. She found me because I worked with a nurse named Mark in Vegas. Mark was one of the first members of the Hidden Pack, funnily enough he was from Bryce's old pack. Anyhow, anyone is welcome if they are loyal and treat everyone fairly. No racism, sexism, or any other type of bigotry allowed. We are LGBTQ+ heavy and have quite a few female alphas as well. We pay what we can into the pack dues, don't demand a huge percentage like other packs or disqualify people or ban them if they can't afford to pay, anyhow, the dues all get used for the pack. Mariam doesn't take a salary. She has a regular job she uses as her source of income. It's amazing. There are also no pack lands, so the dues don't get wasted on property taxes and such. Although I think she'll make sure the taxes for the campground are covered now. We are everywhere. In all fifty states and even a couple of Canadian provinces. We are basically the telecommuting version of a pack."

Beppie took in all the information Gemma gave her and seemed to be processing it while she sipped her hot chocolate. They were silent for a couple of minutes. Finally, Beppie spoke. "That's very progressive. I like it, but don't some of the wolves suffer from touch deprivation? Or do wolves not need touch as much as we do?"

Gemma smiled at Beppie; she was asking smart and important questions. "Yes, we suffer. Most all of us have monthly visits with Joey, a therapist in the pack, and he prescribes touch when it's needed. Everyone has one or two people that they can count on for touch comfort. Or puppy piles as I call it. I have a friend named Genie. She lives about 2 hours from where I was before here. Every two or three weeks we'd have movie weekends and just spend time on the couch with popcorn and pizza and cuddle. She is going to have to find someone new now that I'm up here. I'm actually a little worried about her. Anyways, it's not the same as seeing and touching people every day, but it does the trick."

They spent a little more time talking and enjoying their coffee and talking about things of no import before Gemma finally cleared her throat, put down her coffee and sigh. "Alright, it is time for the business of death. Did the bodies get moved outside?"

Beppie shook her head. "No, Bryce had us leave them in. They're kinda stacked up in the storage room." She made a face like she'd tasted something nasty. "I have no desire to see them again or smell them for that matter. When we were done, I opened the windows and set up box fans pointing outward. Bryce had a couple in the main lodge that he brought over so when you're done with them just take them back to him. He'll have need of them come summer. It gets hot as Hades up here for a couple of weeks in the summer. You'll probably want to buy a few yourself. Or spoil yourself with a window unit."

Gemma smiled. "I will look into it. I'm probably going to have to get an A/C unit. It's best for any medical facility. Most likely I'll look for sales in the next couple of months. Fall sales are great for A/C." She laughed as she stood up. "Thank you so much for helping to bring everything over."

"I sent all the pics to Daniel's phone already while you were getting ready. You can look at those later. The box on the couch has a Ziploc bag that I labeled to match each of them with all their personal belongings. None of them had any real ID, but there was a set of keys and a hotel key card on one dude. I hope it helps." She seemed so worried.

"I'm sure it will. Mariam has a lot of resources within the pack. Including police, doctors, nurses, chemists, you name it. Education and having independent professions are very important in our pack. None of us ever want to be at the mercy of a pack again and Mariam supports us in that. A lot of us, not all, but quite a few, have been put through school by the pack. If there is anything to learn from these bodies or their belongings, then we will find it."

"That is amazing. I wish our pack was more like that. Our Alpha isn't opposed to us getting an education, we just don't have the money. I'm trying to apply for as many scholarships as I can, but I'm probably going to be drowning in student loan debt for the rest of my life." She shrugged her shoulders as if she wasn't upset but they both knew that wasn't true.

"What is it you want to do?"

She gave a shy smile. "SAR tech. Specifically with diving and helicopter training. I'll need to do a lot. I was hoping to start my flight training ahead of time, but I don't think I will have a way of making that happen. I will make it all work though."

"That's a lot of work. What piqued your interest in

search and rescue?" Gemma was genuinely curious. They seemed to have such a sheltered life up here.

"In the summers we get a lot of people coming through to hike and such. That's fine, it's pretty rare that they get lost and even if they do it's not too hard to find them with our enhanced senses, but in the winter, there is a cross country trail that runs just north of here. People like to travel the trail and they camp at night and then come morning continue, it's some sort of extreme cross-country thing. Doesn't sound too fun to me, but whatever, I've never enjoyed cross country skiing. When I was twelve, we had a sudden storm. A man couldn't find his way back to his tent, he was only a few feet away. He was lucky enough to have a GPS beacon and he activated it. I heard the helicopter come and get him. He had some mild frostbite, but he was good. They saved him. I just remember thinking that I wanted to do that." She smiled. "When they came sliding out of the helicopter on ropes it looked like so much fun."

"That's amazing. I think you will be amazing at it too. And let me talk to Daniel. I'm not sure what it takes to train or teach or whatever it is called, but he's a helicopter pilot and we've set up a landing pad here for him." Beppie's eyes grew big as saucers. "And I know I can help you get some of your basic level first aid training done. I'm certified for that. I got the certification for that so I could teach at a women's center near where I was living before. It's from a federal program so it is good in all fifty states. When all this crap with these weird guys cools down, I will call you, ok? I promise."

"Are you serious? That is so amazing!" Beppie jumped up and wrapped her arms around Gemma's shoulders. "I am so glad you guys moved in here. I am so happy to have met you."

Gemma didn't learn anything new with the autopsies of the other bodies they'd brought from town, so she took all the samples and information that had been collected and packaged it, storing it carefully for shipping. With a sigh and a stretch of her back she made her way to the phone and dialed Mariam.

"Hello?" Mariam's voice sounded a little confused.

"Hey Alpha, it's me, Gemma."

"Oh, hi. I thought I stored this number. I forgot. I will this time. Maybe. What's up? Did you finish the autopsies?"

"Yep, that's why I'm calling. I didn't really find anything useful. I have all the samples and their personal effects packaged and ready for you. I thought maybe Sam or Mark and maybe Dave and Tiny would have more luck. I was thinking of sending Daniel over to you with them."

"Hmmm." Mariam seemed to be thinking about it. "Actually, I think maybe we will come out there and see you and the campground. Visit. Show our support for Bryce, meet these hawks. I'm intrigued."

Gemma was glad that Mariam was the type of Alpha that let you ask questions. "You don't think it will look like you are trying to check up on him? Like you don't trust him?"

Mariam didn't seem to take offense at that. "I don't

think so. Bryce and I talked about me coming out there during the first month already. He had already let everyone know I wanted to come out and see the campground and see if there was anything that needed attention from their new pack. I think we covered our bases already. You don't feel like I'm checking up on you, do you?"

Gemma chuckled. "No. Thank you for caring, but no, I am fine. I just didn't want anyone getting their pride hurt. In that case I will keep all the samples stored here for you. Do you think it's safe to dispose of the bodies or should those be stored as well?"

"If you already have all the samples, you think Mark and Sam will need, then go ahead and dispose of them. I trust your judgment in this."

"Great. I'll do that today." Gemma rested her eyes for a moment. "Before I hang up and fall asleep for a million years, I should let you know that I talked to the hawks and with Bryce's permission they have access to me and the clinic. They can come in for appointments and are just asked to donate what they can to cover the cost of supplies and meds and he let them know that bartering was an option. I am of the understanding that bartering happens a lot up here, especially in the winter when the supplies run low. This winter is going to be hard on us because we didn't have spring and summer to fill our pantry and freezer with meat and produce. We have plotted out a large piece of land already for next year's garden, but this year is a wash."

"That seems like a good deal. What things do you think I should bring on this trip? We'll be bringing the SUV, so we'll have space."

Gemma thought about it for a minute or two before answering. "I don't know what everyone else might need, but as far as the clinic is concerned, I think we are pretty set. I have catalogs and can get things delivered into Hawk's Landing. I can't think of anything I need either, but Daniel has been saying something about wanting the donuts from the place by his old house. Can you grab him some? As a surprise for me? I'm sure Adam will know what place he means."

Mariam laughed. "No problem. I know the place, all the Redfoots are obsessed with that place. I'll see you tomorrow sometime."

17

Daniel wasn't sure when the right time to mention it was, but if he waited any longer it would become awkward, so it was now or never.

"Gemma?"

She stopped packing up the small boxes, bags, and containers into the Styrofoam cooler and looked up at him. "What's up?"

"I didn't mention it before, because honestly it's usually not all that important, but I think it might actually be important this time, and so, well, I think I should mention it."

She scrunched her eyebrows in a cute way that she probably would hate to know made her look very young. "Mention what?"

Daniel sighed. "I have an almost ridiculous sense of smell. Like a long running family joke. But just a couple months ago we learned that if we had paid more attention to it, that it could have saved us a lot of trouble. It really is a gift." He looked at her face carefully to see if she was going to laugh at him. She didn't, instead she raised her eyebrows in interest.

"Why are you mentioning this now?"

"Well, you see, I think I can tell you what kind of shifters all of these men are. From what I understand we have very limited exemplars to compare so unless they're wolf, hawk, fox, or jaguar it's almost impossible to know what they are."

"Are you saying you think we have more than the four we know about here?" Now her face showed pure interest.

"Definitely. I'm almost certain that at least one of the men is a bear. I probably won't be able to narrow down the type of bear, but who knows. I need to spend some time with the bodies before we burn them. And concentrate."

Gemma slowly continued putting the items into the cooler and slowly tilted her head to the side as if she was thinking. She suddenly stopped. "I should wait to pack these then, because if you can tell what they are we should add that information, actually I will just add it to the inventory list I put on the top. Alright. So, let's have breakfast, I'll get everyone to leave you alone and let you do your thing. Then after all that, we will burn the bodies. Sound good?" She looked up at Daniel with a smile on her face. A real smile, not a pity smile or one of complacency, but a genuine smile.

"That sounds great. And Gemma, thank you for not thinking I'm crazy."

"Why would I think that?"

"Everyone in my family has pretty strong gifts and I was given a strong sense of smell, it's kind of a running joke in my family, and anyone I've told outside of the family has usually just acted like I was an idiot." He admitted quietly.

Gemma huffed. "Well, that's just rude." She finished getting everything stored in the cooler and taped it closed. "Where is Kyle? I was going to ask him to take this over to the main lodge for me, they have a deep freeze over there, but I haven't seen him since I woke up. I feel horrible for not noticing until now."

Daniel smiled at the look of horror on her face. "Don't feel bad, you've had mates for less than a week. I'll take the cooler over to the lodge. Kyle walked his sister and the pups over to her cabin and is helping her and Tabitha get settled and cleaning up the mess the bad guys made. It involved trading beds with multiple people to get the right configuration. It's an entire thing he's doing for them. He shouldn't be too much longer. But he loves cuddling with those pups so it might take a little longer than necessary."

For a moment Gemma lost her smile.

Daniel noticed and pulled her into a hug. "Don't do that. You know as well as I do that we are made for each other. We spent plenty of time convincing Kyle of that. Do we need to convince you too?"

"But I don't think I can have pups. I have never met a dual breed shifter that had pups."

"That doesn't mean that you can't, honestly, how many have you met? And how many were women? Can you shift to both forms or just one? Could they shift into both forms or just one? Did they even want to have pups? Were they sexually active? Did they have fated mates? Did they..."

She cut him off with a laugh "I get it, I get it, I can't know for sure. I will do some more thinking and studying on it."

"Good." He leaned down and gave her a kiss. The kiss quickly deepened, soon they were both panting and there was an obvious tent in his sweatpants. "You are perfect for me. For us. Don't doubt it. Please."

She smiled sweetly at him and wrapped her arms tighter around his neck. "Make love to me. Now. Before someone comes in demanding my time, or some idiots come attacking, or some other absurd thing. Just make me feel good. Right now."

He smiled down at his beautiful mate and pushed his fingers into her hair, firmly grabbing, but not hurting her, and doubling the energy of their kiss. Soon their kissing wasn't enough, and he grabbed her under her ass and picked her up. He wanted to walk her somewhere close but the exam rooms were filled with the bodies of men that had wanted them dead, so he carefully and quickly turned and made his way toward the stairs.

Daniel was startled to see Kyle leaning against the front door smiling at them. He recovered quickly and winked at his mate and continued to the stairs. He heard Kyle following behind them. He made his way to their bed and lay her down.

She was wearing entirely too many clothes.

Fortunately, she was of the same opinion as him. As soon as she was down on the bed, she released his neck and ripped the sweatshirt off of her head. She wasn't wearing a bra. Her small breasts didn't really require one. Daniel was simply staring at how beautiful his mate was when he felt arms snake around his waist. "Fuck. She is the most beautiful woman I've ever seen. Like something I should write sonnets about, or paint, or sculpt. She should be immortalized." Kyle's voice was nearly reverent.

Daniel could feel how beautiful Kyle thought Gemma was. His substantial cock was hard and teasing Daniel's ass. "Make love to her, Daniel. She needs you."

Damn. Just hearing Kyle say that made Daniel's cock even harder. Gemma was wiggling and squirming to get her yoga pants and socks off. Fortunately, she'd kicked her sneakers off somewhere on the stairs. Daniel quickly followed suit and soon they were both naked. He could hear Kyle getting undressed behind him, but the sight in front of him held his attention and he couldn't look away. Gemma, beautiful Gemma, with one hand pinching and rolling her nipple while the other was rubbing her pussy. Her eyes, pupils blown, were staring straight into his. She wanted him and wanted him to know it. It was beautiful.

He wanted her so badly that it hurt.

He almost jumped when he felt Kyle rub his hand down him slowly, caressing every inch of his back from shoulder to the bottom of his ass. It felt so good. A simple touch that had Kyle throwing his head back and grabbing the base of his cock to stave off his orgasm.

"I am so close. Please. I want to hold off." He didn't know what he was asking. Or even who he was asking. He just knew that he was too close.

Gemma smiled at him, the smallest barely there smile and he couldn't take it anymore. He pounced. Kneeling on the floor next to the bed and pulling her towards the edge.

Wrapping both arms under her legs he lifted her hips and brought her pussy to his mouth. He needed to show her how much he wanted her. He had never wanted to love on someone so much as he did right now. He had always loved pleasing his partners. But it had never been something that felt as important as taking his next breath until he met Gemma and Kyle. He didn't know what he would do without them. Without holding them and loving them. He kissed her long and deep, rolling her clit with his tongue. He looked up to see her playing with her nipples, rolling them between forefingers and thumbs. Pinching them a little harder than he would ever attempt, he'd be too worried about hurting her.

He continued to make love to her with his mouth, long deep strokes, short flicks of his tongue, nibbles and teases with his lips, finally releasing her hips with his right hand so he could use his fingers to bring her even more plea-sure. He felt Kyle kneel on the floor behind him. He was so close and warm behind him. It felt so good. He was also naked, his cock firmly notched between Daniel's checks without trying to fuck him. Kyle reached his right hand around, sliding it right along Daniel's. "Use me, use my fingers too."

Just hearing his words made Daniel thrust his ass back onto Kyle. "Sorry."

Kyle kissed the side of his neck. "No, don't say sorry, if I didn't want to participate I wouldn't have followed. I will never be offended by you wanting me. Either of you. I might not respond how other people would, but I won't be offended by my mates wanting me, that's a gift."

Their fingers intertwined and Daniel sighed. He took Kyle at his word and let the stress of the moment go. Doubling his efforts with his mouth. Daniel took their intertwined fingers and brought them to Gemma's pussy. He started by simply using one of Kyle's fingers and sliding it deep inside of her. Soon she was lifting her hips and begging for more. They gave her more. When they each had two fingers pumping in and out of her, she came and while her body pulsed around their fingers Daniel couldn't stand it any longer. "I need her, Kyle, please." He wasn't sure why he'd said that. It felt right.

"Make love to our mate. Show her how much you want her."

Daniel didn't have to be told twice. He eased their fingers out and stood. He slid her up on the bed so there would be room and climbed up to join her. Her eyes were glassed over, lips swollen and red, hair a mess and breath coming in short pants. She was beautiful. She reached her hands out to him and smiled. "Please mate. I need you."

Sliding his arms under hers and grabbing her shoulders from beneath he lined himself up and slid in, one deep long push. They groaned together at that first perfect feeling of bliss. But soon it wasn't enough, and Daniel had to move. He wasn't in a hurry now though. He'd already made sure she'd had an orgasm, he wanted to make sure he was thorough and gave her another. He slowly made love to her, driving deep and filling her completely. Making love to her was like heaven.

There was the unmistakable sound of lube being opened somewhere behind him, the snick that always made his ass clench and dick get hard. Just hearing that made him thrust harder and deeper, Gemma crying out and scratching her nails down his back.

He jumped when he felt Kyle's hand touch the top of his ass. "Shhhh" Kyle's other hand came up and rubbed soft circles on Daniel's shoulders. "I just want to make you feel good." It took a minute and it caused him to lose his rhythm momentarily, but he was finally able to relax. Once again, he was making love to Gemma and that lubed up hand was making its way towards his ass. It surprised him when Kyle didn't immediately try to finger him, but instead used those slicked fingers to roll and caress his balls. Daniel threw his head back

"Fuck, that feels so good. You're going to make me…. I'm not ready to yet."

Kyle chuckled. It sounded almost evil. He moved away from Daniel's balls and finally started rubbing slow small circles around his tight hole. He was matching his movements with Daniel's, and it was hypnotic and erotic. Finally, just when he was about to come, Kyle sank his middle finger deep into Daniel's ass. It took his breath away for a second. But it felt so fucking good. Kyle knew what he was doing with that finger and soon one became two. Daniel was chasing his orgasm now. He needed it but he wasn't sure how to get it. When he sank into Gemma it felt so good, and her arms wrapped around him so tightly, her legs wrapped around him and Kyle both, but when he pulled back his breath caught, and he would shake with pleasure as those fingers pegged him right in the prostate. Fuck. He didn't know what he wanted more. He didn't know what feeling to chase. Daniel was getting desperate, then those fingers abandoned him.

"No, please…"

"Shhhh.. I have you." Kyle kissed between his shoulder blades and then Daniel caught his breath as his body was forced deep into Gemma by the force of Kyle's cock filling him completely. "You are so good to me Daniel. You make me feel so good."

Then Daniel didn't have to think or worry at all.

Didn't have to decide what felt better or how fast or slow to go, how to please Gemma or if he was going to come too soon. He was the person being loved on and being used for Kyle to make love to them both at the same time. It felt so good. Daniel never wanted it to end. But sooner than he liked it did. First Gemma came, her walls pulsing around him were too much to withstand and in a rush and a shout he came, deep and hard and Kyle fucked him through it. He kept fucking him even after he was too sensitive and was whining and almost begging, and finally Daniel felt Kyle freeze deep inside him and fill him up.

Kyle went to the restroom and, turning on the sink, cleaned himself off first and then grabbed a couple of washcloths, getting them wet with warm water and returning to their bedroom. He carefully used one to wipe down Gemma, she didn't even move. Of course, she had only had a couple hours nap instead of a full night's sleep. Then he took the other and carefully wiped off Daniel's cock which made the man whine a little then he rolled him a bit and swiped between his cheeks. Daniel was blushing but Kyle was going to get him cleaned up before they fell asleep. And Kyle wanted them to fall asleep for a bit of a nap if nothing else.

He walked back to the restroom and rinsed out the cloths before hanging them over the edge of the hamper. He made his way back to the room and climbed into the bed, keeping Daniel in the middle. Daniel kept his back to him, and Kyle wasn't sure why. He pulled the blanket up over them all and wrapped his arm around Daniel.

He flinched. Kyle felt ill. He took his hand back. He knew there was a reason he didn't usually like sex. He was obviously bad at it and shouldn't do it. He sighed.

"I'm sorry." He didn't know what else to say. He'd obviously hurt Daniel, his mate. That was the last thing he wanted to do.

"What?" Daniel actually sounded confused.

"I know I'm not any good at this, but I didn't think I'd hurt you, I figured I'd fumble a little or do something embarrassing but I never in a million years meant to hurt you." Kyle hated himself a little right now.

Daniel didn't say anything, just buried his face a little more into the pillow.

"Don't do that Daniel." Kyle hadn't realized Gemma was awake. And he wasn't following her words. "Can't you hear it in his voice? Feel it through our connection? He's beating himself up for hurting you. Tell him the truth. Don't make both of you suffer for something that is a non-issue."

Daniel's head snapped up at the last words. "What do you mean 'non-issue'? I should just be fine with the fact that suddenly I like to be told what to do? I've never liked that before. I've always been in charge. And that's only in the rare case it wasn't completely vanilla. And I've never let anyone make me hurt before. Ever. Why would I do that?" He was a little angry now.

Kyle was confused. Instead of trying to fake it, he admitted it freely. "I don't know what's happening."

Gemma sighed and snuggled deeper into her pillow. She really was exhausted. "Daniel is upset. With himself, not with you. He let you tell him what to do. He likes you teasing him and dragging his pleasure out. He liked that you kept fucking him even after he came and it kind of hurt, and he liked that you made him hurt. He probably never let that happen before. But he's letting his pride make him hurt you because he's confused."

Daniel sat up a little. "That's not fair. I'm not trying to hurt him. I'm just… I don't… I'm… FUCK." He sat up all the way and flipped the covers off, sliding himself down the bed and off he made his way to the bathroom. At the last minute he stopped and turned. He looked them both in the eyes and took a breath. "I am not mad or upset with either of you. Nobody did anything wrong. I'm just a little confused and need a minute. Nothing is wrong with how I felt, nothing is wrong between consenting adults ever, I just have to reevaluate who I thought I was in the bedroom. That sounds fucking dumb when I say it out loud. I'm taking a shower and then I'm going to go down and sniff dead guys."

Kyle didn't know what to do with that. He heard the shower turn on. He looked over to Gemma. "Should I go talk to him?"

She smiled at him and shook her head. "No, let him think. Come give me some cuddles. I just had mind blowing sex with my mates and I'd like some love and cuddles now."

Kyle smiled. "I can do that."

He was the big spoon to her little spoon and it felt good. Even though they were naked and his cock rested against her perfect ass, he didn't get hard or feel the need to make love to her again. And yes, he considered what they did making love to both of them. He wondered…

"When we are all together like we just were, do you

consider it that we're all making love? That sentence wasn't very clear. Hold on. Like I was just thinking that you and I had just made love, even though biologically..."

Gemma started laughing. "Stop! Yes, I understand. And yes, in my opinion you and I just made love too." She turned over so they were facing each other now.

"I was just wondering. I know my ideas about sex are not the same as everyone else. I'm actually surprised at how much sex I've wanted since meeting you guys."

Gemma nodded her head. "I was going to ask you about that. I know that you said you're ace, but what does that mean? Wait, that made me sound like an idiot. I mean, what does it mean specifically to you? I know that it's different for everyone. That it can be almost a kind of spectrum. What do we need to know for you, to understand you better?"

"Wait for me!" Daniel called from the shower. "I'm coming right now." Shifter hearing was a gift sometimes.

The water turned off and in just a moment Daniel was back in the bedroom with a towel wrapped around his waist. He looked at both of them a little sheepishly and dropped his towel. He crawled into bed on the other side of Kyle, cuddling up behind him.

"I'm sorry I flipped out. It was my issue, not yours and I'm really, really sorry I made you feel bad. You did nothing wrong, and I just needed a minute to wrap my head around everything. I'm aware that people are ever evolving and that there is never anything wrong between people when they are consenting. But for whatever reason what we did confused me for a minute. I'm hoping I'm over it. I can't promise that I'll never flip out again. I can promise that if I don't like something or want you to stop that I will always tell you. Always. I may be a little confused. But I'm never going to let someone do something I don't like, so please don't ever worry about that. Is that something you can understand or deal with? That I'm a flake and don't know myself as well as I thought?" Daniel looked over at Kyle with uncertain eyes.

Kyle smiled at him. "Of course. This is all new to us. All of us. Just like you I am learning more about myself too. I'm not comfortable with all of it but both of us can work on it together, right?"

Daniel smiled back. "Right. Now, getting back to what Gemma was asking you. Explain it to us both. I don't want to mess up."

"Well, that's kinda complicated, even to me." He sighed, scrubbed a hand over his face and continued. "I never crave sex. Like ever. I masturbate occasionally maybe once a year or so and usually because I feel like a freak because of something someone has said so I think to myself 'maybe they're right, maybe I have to do this' and I do it and it's fine. I orgasm and it works. It's not like I hate orgasms, it's nothing like that, shit, it's so freaking confusing." He sighed again. "I enjoy it when it's happening. I loved what we did. I wouldn't have joined in if I didn't want to. When we are together in bed, I am 100% there with you. I am totally enjoying everything and want to play and fuck and lick and all the fun. But if I hadn't seen you and smelled your desire and tasted your lust in the air, I wouldn't have thought about it or missed it. I am also very Demi. I have to have a connection. Maybe Demi isn't the right word, I don't know. I know that if we had met and decided to date but weren't fated that there is no way I would have slept with you yet. I would've needed more time to get to know you. I think our mating link will make me want to make love with you guys a lot more often than I would've with anyone else. Because I can feel your desire. I still don't know what that will mean for us." Daniel scooted himself a little closer and wrapped his arms around Kyle, spooning him.

"Is this alright?" Kyle gave him a small kiss on the back of his neck.

"Yes. Please. I love touch. This is another thing that has caused problems in the past." While he spoke, Gemma pulled herself closer to his front, resting her cheek against his chest and using her top hand to rub and stroke long lines down his chest and as far as she could reach, to the bottom of his hip, and back again. "I would want to touch, lay on the couch and watch a movie while we cuddle, and rub and stroke, but they always assumed it was foreplay. It wasn't, I just wanted the touch. I need it. I need to feel your skin against mine. I need you."

Kyle was almost embarrassed at the raw need he heard in his own voice. But if he couldn't be honest with his own mates then he had no hope. And he wanted to show Daniel that there was never any reason for him to feel shame like he did earlier.

He didn't know if it was their link or just Daniel's intuition, but he seemed to know what Kyle was thinking. "Don't be ashamed or ever feel like you need to hide your need from us. We saw what happened earlier when I tried to hide my feelings. It almost caused a disaster. We are literally fated for each other, which means there is nothing that one of us could want or need that the others wouldn't be able to give or crave giving." He was abruptly quiet, but Kyle could tell he wasn't done speaking. He looked down at Gemma and knew she would wait for Kyle to continue as well. They quietly lay in the bed, all just petting each other and breathing in the scent of each other while they waited for Daniel to be ready to finish his thought. Finally, he took a deep breath and spoke quickly, almost like he thought if he said it fast no one would hear him. "When you told me what to do and kind of controlled what I was doing and stuff like that, did you like it, or did you just do it just because?"

Kyle didn't answer right away, he could feel that this was an important question, one that mattered. So, he pondered the question and rubbed Daniel's hand that had snuck over onto his belly. "When we were making love, I could feel you both so strongly in my head. I could feel how much Gemma wanted to feel us both making love to her, how she wanted to look up and see both of our faces looking down at her with love and lust in our eyes. I could feel that she was completely in love with the idea of me fucking you into her. And knowing that she wanted that made me want it and it made me so hard and so excited. But before that your lust filled me. Your lust tastes so much different than hers. It started so powerful and strong and just ... I guess the word would be dominant? But then I felt your need and I wanted to fill your need. I wanted to sate it. Then I started touching you and something about making you moan and….squirm?… felt good to me. Too good. It made me so hard. It made me want things I don't usually want. So, I took. And every time I felt you surrender and do what I wanted, it made me feel more, more… I don't know the word. I just know I wanted more. I wanted to feel you bend to me. I could feel it when I kept pushing you after you came. You were shaking and I could tell it was maybe not painful, but definitely something on that side of the board. I know what it feels like when you keep touching yourself after, it almost hurts, it's too sensitive. Fuck. I loved knowing I was forcing you to feel that. And even better, I loved knowing that you could've pushed me off at any time if you'd wanted to, but you let me keep pushing you and making you hurt. It made me come so hard knowing that. It's making me hard right now just thinking about it." He took the hand he was holding and slid it down to his thick cock that was resting firmly along his belly now. "Touch me." He hoped this was what Daniel wanted. It felt right, it felt like what he wanted too, but Kyle was also so scared that he was doing the wrong thing. What did he know? Daniel slowly started stroking his cock, softly, from tip to root. Too softly. "Harder baby, let me feel you." Daniel tightened his grip, almost too tight and it felt amazing. He continued to stroke slowly and firmly. Gemma's body moved away from him, and he furrowed his brow at her and she just smiled as she reached to the nightstand and grabbed their lube. She quickly rolled back closely and opened the container. She dripped a few cold drops directly onto his cock and Daniel's hand. Kyle sighed as the tight grip started a smoother slide, which made it so much better. He started to throw his head back but before he could he was distracted by Gemma dripping more lube on his thigh, the one he was laying on. She took her own top leg and put it over his large thigh, now wet with lube, pushing his top leg back some, into Daniel's space. She started a slow grind.

"I love your leg hair, it's an odd combination of course

and soft somehow, feels so good on my clit." Her hips started moving faster.

"Daniel, stroke me faster, and tighter." He did as he was told. "Good boy." Kyle reached back his arm and pulled Daniel's body flush against his own ass and leg. He didn't let go; he knew somehow that Daniel wanted to be held tight. "Rub off on me baby, let me feel you come on me." Daniel's hand stuttered for a moment. Kyle knew he was still struggling but Kyle hoped seeing Gemma humping on him from the other side would show him there was nothing to be embarrassed about. Slowly but surely, Daniel started rubbing his cock on Kyle's firm ass. He matched his hand strokes to the motions of his hips. Soon enough, both Daniel and Gemma were grinding with a speed and desperation that made Kyle so hard it almost hurt. The taste of their needs was delicious. Daniel's cock was leaking so much that it nearly felt as if he'd already come. Kyle looked over his shoulder at Daniel "Slide that big dick between my cheeks baby." Kyle stuttered again in his movements. "Just between my cheeks. I'm not ready for more." Daniel nodded and reached down to do as he was told. "Get me all wet." Before Daniel could strain himself to find the lube Gemma reached over and squeezed the bottle over Kyle's ass. Daniel slid his cock between Kyle's cheeks easily and sighed with the pleasure of it.

"Don't get lazy, squeeze my cock, make me feel good, baby."

Daniel whined, but the feelings Kyle got from him were good ones, he was enjoying himself and he clamped down on Kyle's cock and it took his breath away.

Once again, they started a beautiful writhing dance,

Gemma rubbing herself against Kyle's hard thigh while Daniel's hand was squeezing him almost too hard. Kyle's real pleasure was coming from the feeling of bliss radiating from his mates. Especially from Daniel. Kyle didn't think Daniel had ever let himself dive into this side of his needs. He could feel his hard cock sliding between his cheeks. He knew he might want to feel that cock inside of him one day, but he wasn't ready for that yet, if he ever would be.

Suddenly, Gemma seemed to double her efforts. She reached her arm over and grabbed onto Daniel's arm. Her short, perfect nails digging into his sun kissed skin. He was going to wear her marks for a while. That thought made Kyle excited. He thrust his top leg up and over onto Gemma hard and bent down to give her a kiss. At the same time, he let go of Kyle's ass just long enough to spread some of the extra lube from his own body onto his hand. He brought that hand back to Daniel's ass and without warning started pressing a single digit into Daniel's tight hole. Kyle almost lost his composure just remembering how good that hold felt snug around his cock last night, but he managed to hold on. He didn't have to wonder if Daniel wanted it or not, his sweet boy lifted his top leg and lay it on top of Kyle's, never stopping his thrusting and trying his best to keep a constant flow and squeeze with his hand. He quickened his movements and forced his finger deeper into Daniel's sweet hole. Fuck. It was like velvet inside. He sought out that sweet spot and knew by the gasp when he'd found it. He was relentless, never-ending rubbing and tapping and rubbing some more. He needed to make this man crazy. He had to give up too soon, the angle was all wrong and he was getting a cramp. He sighed and looked over his shoulder at Daniel. "Finger yourself."

Daniel whimpered but did as he was told. He let go of Kyle's cock and used that hand to start fingering his ass.

The sounds they all were making was music to Kyle's ears. He never knew. He was enjoying the touch and knew he'd love the orgasm he might have, he didn't know if they'd ever truly understand how the rest, the intimacy, the control of Daniel, the desperation in Gemma's eyes, the love radiating off of both of them, the closeness they were sharing and the flow of their mating link… this was what he craved, the thing he'd be seeking when he would say he was horny or needy. This. This complete …completeness.

His thought was interrupted by the sweet sound of Daniel begging "please, please, please. I need to come. Please can I come, please. I'm going to come. I want to be good; I want to… please."

He couldn't help it; it was too good. "No. Wait for Gemma to come first."

The sound Daniel let out was almost enough to push Kyle over the edge even without touching his cock, it did for Gemma she started shaking and he could feel her sweet juices flowing down his thigh. Daniel increased his speed and kept fucking his ass with that finger. It was a sweet torture for both of them. Kyle loved hearing Daniel's soft whimpers. Kyle wasn't sure how long he would've continued to torture the sweet boy, but he finally said something that pushed Kyle over the edge. An edge Kyle didn't know he had.

"Please, please….alpha!"

He exploded. He came like he'd never come before.

And right behind him was Daniel spraying his sweet load all over his ass and hole.

It took a while for them to stop gasping for breath and have the ability to function again. When they did finally recover Kyle carefully extracted Gemma then rolled to his back and dragged Daniel up on top of him. He placed his hands on either side of his face and gave him a soft and sweet kiss. The kind you see on Christmas specials or that teenagers dream about.

"Don't ever be ashamed of what you need again. And neither will I." Daniel didn't respond at first, so Kyle spoke again. "Hey. I'm serious. We both have discovered things about ourselves today. Things we didn't know but that are part of us and part of what we need and desire. We can't live our lives ashamed. Do you understand?"

Daniel answered but it was quiet and nearly unintelligible.

"Not good enough. Do. You. Understand. Me. Mate? Or do you need to be punished?" Daniel's eyes opened wide, and he nodded.

"Yes, I understand."

Kyle may have only just realized what he needed in his life, but he'd spent years studying all sorts of BDSM and porn looking for something or anything to get him excited. Who knew all that research would come in so handy?

He looked over at a very sleepy Gemma. "How are you feeling about all of this, love?"

"I don't need an alpha. But I like being bossed around sometimes, a little. You'll know when. I'm not subtle. But what I really like is watching you be in charge of Daniel's. It makes me very, very wet."

Daniel and Kyle smiled at their sweet mate.

Kyle held out his hand. "Come give us some kisses before we get up and take showers and we have to be responsible adults again."

She slid over to the two men with a smile on her face.

19

After a little nap and a long shower Daniel finally made his way downstairs to do what he'd set out to do much earlier in the day. Kyle had already left with the cooler to take over to the deep freeze. Gemma followed him in, holding a yellow notepad and a pen. He was a little embarrassed to do this, it was starting to feel like a party trick, but maybe for the first time in his life his gift would be useful for more than hunting season.

Daniel made his way to the first body which was covered with a simple sheet on the examination table. He quickly got to business. He leaned close to the man's neck and took a deep and thorough breath through both his mouth and nose. This one was easy. "Wolf. But from the North."

She stopped what she was writing and looked up at him with a question on her face. "How can you tell he's from the north?"

Daniel shrugged. "I guess that's not technically accurate. But snowy animals have a different scent. So, he might not be from the north but he's a snowy wolf of some sort."

Gemma smiled and shook her head. "That is amazing." She finished writing and looked back at him with expectation on her face.

"It might be something you already noticed during the autopsy, but they recently had elk." He shrugged and moved to the next body which was laying on the floor. He repeated the action, squatting near the body and leaning in close to breath in the smell of him. He was about to blurt out deer but stopped himself and took another deep breath, closing his eyes and concentrating. "I'm only mostly sure on this one but I would have to say he's an elk shifter. That makes their last meal creepier somehow."

"Huh." She wrote on the page again and made some notes.

They continued the process for quite some time. There were a few bodies he was unsure of and had to come back to but when they were finally finished there were only two, he couldn't positively place.

"All I know is that he smells very much like a type of bird, but also reminds me of something kind of almost tropical maybe. And that guy seems very cold weather like and maybe bearish... but not. Actually, he reminds me of a scent I caught off of Elkan once that he said was a friend from the club, but that's not very helpful. Sorry."

Gemma nudged him with her shoulder. "Are you kidding? Eight of Ten you knew and four of those I'd never even heard of. I mean... come on. I didn't even realize there were crocodile shifters."

Daniel smiled. He liked being helpful. He really felt

that for the first time his gift was truly being used. His sisters had used theirs multiple times to help people find mates. His brothers all had different gifts they'd used to help the pack in a variety of ways, but he always felt like he was kind of useless. Maybe he wasn't useless after all.

"All right, let's call over to the lodge and let Bryce know we can get rid of these bodies now. I'm done having them in my clinic."

They turned and walked out of the storage room. Both of them quickly stepped back into the restroom to wash their hands with the medical grade soap.

"I want to take a shower and get the smell off, but I know we are going to have to help carry them all out anyhow and then the smoke…." Daniel sighed. "We'll just have to wait until everything is done tonight."

Gemma smiled at him. "You'll survive. You might not like it, but you'll be fine.

When they made their way to the kitchen, they found Kyle waiting for them with a smile. "People are coming now to help us. We will get this nastiness done then we will join everyone in the lodge. A lot of the hawks stayed to help and when we're all done there is going to be a big dinner for everyone while we let the clinic air out some more. Sound good?"

Before either of them could answer, there was a knock at the front door before it opened a crack and a voice called out, "Safe to come in?" It was Bryce.

Daniel smiled and hollered "Come on in Bryce." For his mates he added in a softer voice. "Sounds good, and when all that's done, I'd love to cuddle in bed with a movie?"

The three shared a smile.

Bryce was busy showing the others in. It was a large collection of shifters, both hawks and wolves and Daniel was glad for the help. He didn't want to touch the bodies any more than he already had. He was happy to see that so many had come, that he only had to help with one of the bodies.

Bryce stopped to speak with them before leaving. "A couple of people are coming right now to help you three get this place sanitized while we take care of the bodies. As soon as you're done make sure and open all the windows then just join us all over at the lodge. We have a lot of food over there; it should be a nice dinner. And I think after we eat all of us will want to have some serious conversation about everything that happened. Including the hawks, I know they have questions too."

Daniel nodded. "Sounds good. We will get started now and see you in a bit."

Daniel followed Kyle and Gemma into the storage room to get the cleanser she wanted them to use, he wasn't going to try to guess the right stuff.

"When we're done with the tables, we will need to do the floors too."

By the time she was done talking there were a few more people there to offer their assistance. Gemma gave them some instructions and they all got to work. It didn't take long, and they had the place as clean as it could get. The smell lingered and they walked around opening all of the windows in each and every room of the clinic and even the ones upstairs in their private space. The rooms downstairs still had the fans blowing outward and they left them like that. Fortunately, there was a nice breeze happening outside as well.

Daniel really hoped it smelled better by the time they got back.

20

Kyle didn't like the energy in the room. They were simply sitting and enjoying the variety of food that had been provided but he could feel the anger and fear in the air like a pot of noodles about to boil over.

He looked up and made eye contact with Daniel. The look in his mate's eyes was enough for him to know that they were both feeling the same thing. He looked around the room looking for Gemma, she'd eaten her food quickly and was already talking to a lot of the older hawks that were here. Kyle knew that she had wanted to visit with them all when they were at the picnic yesterday and hadn't been able to when the day had been cut short. But he didn't like her being so far away from him and Daniel.

"We're being overprotective. Even if something went wrong right now, there is a room full of wolves here that wouldn't let anything happen to her." Daniel reached his hand over and placed it on top of his. He smiled at his mate.

"Thank you. I know that logically, but I still am feeling so nervous and anxious." Kyle admitted.

"My mom and dad say that it takes time for our wolves to calm down after mating. That for a while it is hard for us to let our mate, or mates in our case, do anything without us hovering."

Kyle sighed. "Great. Because Gemma totally seems like the type of woman that likes to be smothered." Daniel laughed loud and long.

"Well, at least we kind of have a reason this time. There is some actual shit going down, this isn't just our wolves being all overbearing and macho. She probably is just as worried but just better at hiding it cause she's more evolved and shit." He smiled at Kyle with that crooked little smile that made him want to wrap him up and cuddle him all night.

Kyle gasped. "Did you just try to distract me with your sexy man smile?"

Daniel laughed again. "Depends, did it work?"

Kyle gave him his best look of authority. "Don't tease me in public, it's not nice boy."

Daniel's gulp was audible.

"Are you two having fun without me? Not fair." Gemma leaned down, giving Daniel a soft kiss before sitting down next to Kyle and giving him one too. She rested her head on his shoulder and sighed. "Bryce said they're about to start. He's grabbing the hawk Alpha, Jeremy, and they'll be leading the discussion. I think they're both getting more coffee first."

Daniel and Kyle both nodded.

Gemma seemed tired. No. More than that. She seemed weary. To the bone and fully worn out. Kyle wrapped his arm around her shoulder and pulled her closer to him. "Are you ok? You've had a very full week of excitement and crazy and scary. What do you need?"

She sighed, her breath ruffling the collar of his button up shirt. "I think I just need rest. Especially since I'm pretty sure we are going to have a little baby boom next month." She rubbed her face into his chest and neck, more like a cat than the wolf she was. "I'm so tired. I've been so tired for so long."

He was going to comment and reassure her but before he had the chance Bryce's booming voice interrupted them. He rose from his seat and started the meeting.

"Attention everyone. Can I get your attention? Go ahead and keep eating but we are going to start. A lot has happened in the last 24 hours, and we need to talk about it. We are lucky enough to be forging a friendship with the hawk's and I want to welcome them all here tonight and a special welcome to their Alpha who is sitting here with me."

The man gave a slight nod from where he sat.

"Alpha Mariam will be here tomorrow to go over any questions or concerns that we still have after tonight.

The first thing we know is that we were attacked. All of the attackers said very little if any at all, but we have pieced a lot of it together. What it amounts to is some sort of racist bullshit, excuse my French. Before we make any assumptions or accusations, I think we can agree we need more information. I don't want any of us jumping the gun on this. Our Alpha will be here tomorrow and I'm hoping she has more information than I do." There was a little bit of whispering chatter when he referred to his Alpha as a her. "I know for a fact that she has more access to labs and forensics and all that science stuff you see on the tv, so we will wait to find out as much as we can. For now, we want everyone to be diligent. Don't go anywhere alone. Keep yourselves in groups and keep your eyes open. Keep the pups, and um… other kids, under watchful eyes. We are all worried that these weren't the last of them.

"What if more of them come because of you?" The voice was from the rear of the room. A hawk that Kyle hadn't managed to get the name of at the picnic. If he remembered correctly then he had been one of the men manning the barbecue and laughing with the others before all hell broke loose.

The hawk Alpha stood. "Who else feels this way? Either hawk or wolf? A few scattered hands rose, and the Alpha and Bryce looked at each other and nodded. "Alright. Let's leave everyone to enjoy their food. Those of you with concerns, come outside with us, we need help gathering wood and starting the fire. We're going to have s'mores in a bit. Come on gang."

Daniel was surprised when Bryce asked him to accompany the group outside. "I'm not used to having to report back to anyone, I don't want to forget something important because I didn't realize it was important at the time."

It made sense and Daniel was pretty impressed with how well Bryce was doing with his change in position. He had assumed the man was going to be upset when he actually seemed more relieved than anything else.

Daniel could tell the Alpha and Bryce were both feeling a lot of stress, but they were good at their jobs and didn't scream or hit or make anyone pay for speaking up against them.

Bryce broke the silence. "Since we haven't been here in years, there is a lot of dead wood everywhere. In fact, we are doing us all a favor getting it all gathered up. We don't want to leave kindling laying all around with bonfire season coming. You know all the kids are going to be making them whether we tell them it's alright or not."

The Alpha joined in. "You have a lot of young ones too, right? You call them pups?" They walked and picked up wood while they spoke, just letting the others trail behind and around them.

"Yup. We have, or will have by the first snow, twenty-four pups under two years old. All the cabins have wood burning stoves. Some have been updated to also have propane ovens and stoves, but heat is all wood based. We have some safety grates coming tomorrow with Alpha Mariam that we're going to put up, to make sure the stoves are child safe. Apparently, nobody cared about that in the 70's."

The men chuckled. "Where are we stacking all of this?" The question came from the young man that had raised his concerns inside the lodge.

"We can stock up the pile over there," he pointed to a large, cleared area behind the main lodge. "Then later if we are still talking, we can start loading the piles by the individual cabins, starting with the elderly and the ones who have pups."

"Who decides when we're done talking?" The young man sounded more than a little upset, but not necessarily mad.

"We all do." His Alpha answered. "We need to find a way to live together," he spoke loud enough for everyone to hear. "We don't need to be blaming each other for some bad people attacking all of us. We need to be glad that we've had the luck to find another kettle, um pack, to befriend."

They were silent for a little while and then the young man mumbled something.

The Alpha looked up, "Come again?"

He sighed. "I couldn't get to Dylan."

The Alpha's shoulders dropped, and he set the wood he was holding down. He took the man into his arms and gave him a hug. "Oh Josh." He sighed. "I had him. I grabbed your boy in my very own arms and held him until I handed him to my mate to protect. She made sure. She and the others had all those kids safe. Each and every one, wolf and hawk alike, safe and sound."

"What if…"

"Don't fill your head with what ifs. We are lucky enough to have more than doubled our numbers by gaining friends in the wolf pack. Let's not take that for granted."

Josh nodded his head. Daniel was happy and impressed with the way the hawk Alpha was handling the introduction of a wolf pack to his territory.

Bryce spoke up then. "We are finally seeing that there are other types of shifters, it's like a veil is being lifted off of my eyes. I'm not sure why or what is causing it, but I have a feeling that those goons are of the opinion that we shouldn't be friends. I don't like that much." He sighed. "Hopefully Alpha Mariam will have more information for us tomorrow."

One of the other young men that had come out with them spoke up, he was a wolf, Daniel didn't think they'd ever been introduced. "When my gran was dying, she was one of the lucky ones that died of old age, she was kinda getting a little bit senile. Or whatever our equivalent of that is. Anyhow. She'd tell me stories about how her great grandmother had been rescued by a clan of beasts from the north. She made them sound all scary and big and hairy, they sounded made up. But she said she had fallen into the river when she was out playing one day and they found her, saved her, then took her to a herd of deer to keep her safe until her pack could come and find her, because the wolves and the deers were allies. She was always talking about the big hairy beasts, and deers that were shifters, and we just thought she was crazy, or making up stories. But what if she wasn't? What if, a long time ago, we all knew about each other? Maybe something happened to make us forget?"

They all seemed to think about that for a beat. Finally, Bryce scratched his head and cocked it to the side. "Well, it couldn't have been a disagreement or falling out, our ancestors would've passed down their anger or distaste for other shifters. It's like it's been wiped from our memories all together. Who or what could cause such a thing? That's not natural."

Daniel broke their tense silence. "I really, really hope that Mariam has some answers, because I am getting a very odd feeling about all of this. And it is most definitely not a good feeling. I think Alpha and Bryce are right to keep us together as allies. If someone or something was strong enough to cause this level of memory wipe or whatever we want to call it, then I think we are going to need all the help we can get. I really hope she has some answers."

The group seemed much calmer than when they'd walked out not that long ago. They no longer seemed angry or at odds with each other. The group quickly gathered as much wood as they could, separating by size, a couple of men starting the process of splitting the logs that were too large to stack. The main lodge's wood pile was near to overflowing and many of the smaller cabins were well on their way to having full piles too before people started meandering out of the lodge. The younger people joined in gathering wood and preparing the cabin piles while the older people started their bonfire and began bringing out trays of graham crackers, marshmallows and chocolate for the s'mores.

Soon the group was laughing and enjoying each other's company. Getting to know each other and just having a good time in general. Only the few that had come out earlier seemed to still be wearing the weight of the things they had talked about. As Daniel looked around at them, he started to detect a change in their smell. All of them, from the teenagers to the middle-aged ones, all of the people that had concerns started to smell very similar to the scent he often would catch on his father and uncle after they came home from Elder meetings. It always reminded him of a deep wood scent, but more, it made him think of safety and care. He always remembered thinking that it was the scent of caretakers, watchers, leaders, not just Alpha's but …. guardians.

Jesse and Rena had chosen to drive separately from Mariam, Adam and Ben. They had multiple reasons for this, and most of them were about not wanting to hear the pups cry or smell the desire constantly coming off of Alpha Mariam and her mates whenever they weren't actively thinking about the pups. It was not easy being mated and knowing you couldn't have sex with your mate for more than another year. They rarely got to spend time alone, actually, Jesse could count on his hands the number of times that just he and Rena were alone without a chaperone or the other three of them.

He knew their mating was odd and no one really understood it, but that didn't mean that they didn't all need time alone occasionally. He could admit that he was attracted to Michael and Christian and he even knew he was attracted to Argie, that one he felt he still needed some clarity on. He was planning on bringing the topic up with Rena on the trip but so far, he'd been much more of a chicken than a wolf.

They were almost there. The last sign they passed said they were only about forty miles from Hawk's Landing. Meaning they'd probably be at the camp in a little more than an hour. He'd been reviewing his notes and going over all the different things he'd learned about the multiple varieties of wolves, or shifters in general he was guessing, but he'd let himself get distracted thinking about what to say to Rena.

"You've been thinking pretty hard for a while, you stopped scribbling in your book, and you haven't touched your sketch pad at all. What's up?"

He decided he was never going to find a good way to ask so to just do it. "I know I explained some of the visions that involve all of us, but I have to ask you a question."

"Is this about Argie? About your liking her too?"

His head snapped up so fast he was surprised he didn't get whiplash. Rena giggled.

"It's alright. I've explained before that I can see the connections, and it's kind of amplified if I hold hands with Argie. This means I've seen that we are all connected. I have no need for jealousy, and I know Argie feels the same way. But if any of you are into twin stuff, too bad, that's nasty."

Jesse gulped. Audibly. "But… mates, um…"

She reached over her hand and started to put it on his knee, before she did, she seemed to think twice and asked "Is this alright?" Jesse nodded with a smile. She settled her hand on his knee. "Argie and I had long talks about this. We both agree that we want all of us to be together. We even talked about if it would be weird or gross if we were in the same room or bed if the other one was having sex, if our parents ever allow it, or making out or whatever. We decided that wouldn't bother us, but we have no desire to experiment with each other… I reiterate…. Ew."

Jesse wasn't sure what to say but he was now reciting the different movies starring his favorite actor to try to get his junk under control. No sexy thoughts, no sexy thoughts.

When he felt like he had himself under control again he broke the silence. "I just didn't want you to think that I wasn't dedicated to our mating or that it in any way wasn't enough for me."

She took a moment to answer and was doing that adorable thing with her eyebrows that told him she was thinking. "Do you feel like I am less dedicated to you because I have feelings and desires for Mickey and Chris?"

"No." He answered quickly and honestly.

She gave him a look that clearly said he wasn't seeing the big picture. He sighed and then chuckled. "OK, I see your point." They drove a little longer in silence. "And my attraction to Michael and Christian? That doesn't bother you?" He spoke those words a little quieter and his heart was beating just a little harder.

She put on the blinker and pulled over at a small turn out. She carefully put the old Honda in park and then turned a little in her seat to look at his face.

"Please don't ever compare me or Argie, or even our family to the asinine pack you came from. It doesn't bother me that Adam is mated to a man and a woman. Elkan is mated to a man. And I'm pretty sure we're about to meet Daniel's new mates, from what I overheard, also a man and a woman. So, what about all that would make you think that it would bother me to see the three hottest and nicest and best guys I know be attracted to each other, and yes, eventually when we meet him I will include our other mate in that sentence."

Jesse leaned his head back on the seat and closed his eyes. Ever since the attack it felt like he was constantly fighting off tears. Joey said it was PTSD and the triggers would come for years, and some might never go away. That he'd be in therapy for ages and that it was going to be hard. But he knew that if he ever wanted a complete relationship, a healthy mating, then he needed to do it. "I'm so scared all the time, Rena. You deserve better. So do all of you. I am not even sure I'll ever be able to actually have sex with you guys. Sure, I like the idea of it, but even when I'm alone and daydreaming and I will be thinking about it and all excited and thinking about how I can't wait, then suddenly BAM, gone, zero desire, sometimes I'll realize what I thought that made me get scared but sometimes I won't. What if I never get it figured out?"

She leaned over and rested her head on his shoulder. "According to your vision you must figure it out at least a couple of times."

He laughed mirthlessly. "Ya, but …"

"No buts, even if you didn't know that some pups were yours, you said you were happy. We were happy. Right?"

"Yes."

"Then don't worry about what we may or may not be able to do in bed. If we are happy then it doesn't matter. We obviously figure out at the very least how to please each other emotionally if not physically. But I think you're selling yourself short. It's been like five minutes since your attack. Let yourself heal. My mom and dad have made sure you have plenty of time for that." She didn't sound pleased about the last and it made him laugh.

"You're right about that." He sighed. "We can go again. I'm ok now."

~

Jessie liked the look of Hawk's landing, of course he'd liked it since the first time he'd seen it, in a vision. Their Alpha was a good man, and now he knew he could tell that to Alpha Mariam and mean it. He grabbed his tablet from the backseat and started scrolling through the pages he'd scanned in this last week. Next to him Rena giggled, "So I guess we are definitely supposed to be here then?"

He chuckled along with her. "Yep. I've been seeing this place since I was nine or ten. Nice town. We will vacation here often in the future. Or at least it felt like vacation in the visions, but who knows, maybe we'll be here working on things for Alpha Mariam, or even living here. It's a little unclear." He finished making his notes on the tablet and closed it up again. "Someone here can help us find him, or they do, I'm not sure, I think it's one of those things that isn't truly decided yet." He paused. "It's not entirely clear."

They made the final turn off onto the dirt road leading to the camp. There were a couple of young wolves, probably about their same age, repainting the large sign that had been faded by weather and years. It still had a large mountain scene in the background, he could tell they were simply touching that up, but over that there had been added large birds flying in and out of the clouds and a wolf peeking out from behind a perfectly painted pine. Below all that in bold blue letters it read "HAVEN" and in a bit smaller print beneath "population as needed".

They pulled up and parked next to the SUV but made sure to stay out of the way of unloading the trailer that the SUV had been pulling. Adam and Ben were already unloading the trailer while Mariam stood talking to Daniel and Bryce, both of whom had a pup in their arms. Those girls were going to be so spoiled.

Jesse quickly jumped out of the car and headed to the trailer to help unload the many boxes and goods they'd brought along. It seemed he wasn't the only person with that idea. A large man that looked like some sort of superhero, with dark skin and braided hair was also helping. When he turned, holding a large box, Jesse got a much better look at his face. Jesse recognized him immediately. He didn't say anything, he had figured out over the years that people don't usually like to be met with "I saw you in a vision", but he knew this man. This was the man that would be holding his hand while he cried because Rena will nearly die. It would be years from now, and she was going to make it through, which was his only excuse for not telling anyone about that vision. Not even his mates. Regardless, he immediately trusted this man.

"Hey there, I'm Kyle. You must be Jesse."

Jesse nodded. "That's me. Nice to meet you Kyle." They didn't continue talking, both having a task at hand. Kyle walked off without another word, just a friendly smile. Jesse started helping with the unloading.

The four of them had the trailer and SUV emptied in no time. Jesse was led to a small cabin with two double beds and not much else, by a hawk that introduced himself as Josh. "Sorry, there aren't a lot of accommodations just yet, but it's clean and should be warm enough tonight. You're lucky enough to get one with a restroom and kitchenette. Some don't even have that. Mostly the young singles are sharing those. Anyone elderly, sick, with pups, or mated got first dibs. In that order. I'm helping Bryce get everyone settled."

"It's great, thank you." Jesse smiled at the shy man. He was older than Jesse but seemed a lot more timid than most.

"I was told you might be needing Wi-Fi. That's a no go up here. Not for three more weeks or something. We put a rush on it, but who knows. Middle of nowhere… Anyhow, if you head into town the diner has free WIFI, password is Kettle. Capital K."

"Thanks Josh"

"No problem. I'm supposed to tell you to head over to the clinic whenever you're ready, then there'll be a bigger pack meeting in the lodge and then this evening the other hawks are coming up to join us for another bonfire. Kettle's turn to bring the s'mores."

"Sounds great."

Without another word Josh left. Jesse realized that the small door that he thought was a closet was actually a very small utilitarian bathroom. He took a quick, not so hot shower, and dressed in a clean set of clothes. He was glad. Driving hours in a car didn't leave the freshest of aromas.

Jesse was just sliding on his shoes when the vision hit. It wasn't the strongest one he'd had lately, but it completely took him by surprise, and he felt himself passing out.

> *The mark on his chest had been there for centuries. But on certain days it was almost as if he could feel the ink burning into his flesh all over again. It always happened that way when he was needed. He didn't know how the magic of the mark worked but he immediately knew that he needed to head east. He'd been enjoying the weather in Alaska, he was more suited to it, but it was time to move on. He had a job to do.*
>
> *Days, it had taken him many days longer than he intended to get here. He just hoped it wasn't too late. That some of them could be saved. He hated when he had to wipe out a group completely. He still felt guilt over the cleansing they had to do on the San Juan Islands. He could smell their bodies burning in his sleep, some nights the screams of the young woke him. He knew he had to do this, but sometimes he doubted... just a little.*
>
> *He watched from behind a large tree while the Kettle and the Pack laughed under the moonlight. From what he could hear it was the first time they'd all gathered together at the campground. He didn't know why he was the only one of his kind here. Usually between six or twelve of them showed up for a group this size. There was no way he would be able to clear out all of this impurity on his own. What was he supposed to do now?*
>
> *As if his mark heard him his chest burned and*

he knew that this was to be left for others to take care of, another group would be coming soon. He needed to go south. To the desert, his animal wasn't happy, but he knew his duty. With one last look at the group, he sniffed and moved deeper into the shadows.

How could one group have wolves, hawks, fae, jaguar and .... Maybe a phoenix... living in harmony. It wasn't right.

"Jesse, wake up, please wake up. I think you hit your head when you fell this time," he could hear Rena's concerned voice but wasn't quite able to respond yet. "I don't care what anyone says, you are not safe alone right now, your visions are coming fast and strong, it's dangerous when you're alone."

He didn't think she really wanted an answer, she was simply venting, but he was trying his best to get his mouth to work. Finally, after what seemed like forever, he croaked out "tablet". Rena rolled her eyes but handed over the tablet after opening his document app and turning on dictation. He quickly recited everything, keeping his eyes closed through it all, his mate was right, he'd hit his head pretty hard. When he was done, he sighed and barely opened his eyes. "I think I need something for the pain. Did mom or Sandra pack us up any of that tea?"

Rena sighed. "Yes, but you will also get your butt up and we are going to the clinic, where we are supposed to be anyhow, I might add, and you will let Doctor Gemma look at your head. It split kinda bad back there. You hit it on the edge of the bed frame."

"Yes, mate." He wasn't going to argue with what was an obviously correct assessment of his injury. He was a dumb teenage boy, but not an idiot.

She smiled down at him. "Thank you." Leaning over she gave him a chaste kiss on the lips then helped him slowly get up. "This walk will probably suck for you, it's not too far but I bet that's throbbing."

Since she didn't seem to need an answer, he didn't provide one, the pounding of drums in his head prevented it anyhow.

23

Gemma was resting comfortably on the couch between Kyle and Daniel. They'd brought in a few extra folding chairs so they all could sit without being too crowded. Bryce and his mate were sitting at the breakfast bar while Mariam, Adam and Ben sat in folding chairs. The twins were lying comfortably in the travel crib that was set up next to the couch. While Gemma wasn't a fan of large groups, she understood that this was a necessary meeting.

When the door opened, she knew that something was wrong immediately. The boy she'd seen earlier looked a bit dazed and as if he had run a marathon, his skin was pale and clammy, there was also a slow trickle of blood running down his neck behind his ear. The young girl spoke up before Gemma could even manage to get out of her seat.

"He passed out again. Hit his head on the edge of the bed this time, he might need a stitch or two. And he's a little wobblier than usual." She sounded upset and

Gemma didn't blame her. From what she understood they were mates.

Daniel and Kyle had jumped up as well and were taking over the duty of helping Jesse. It was a good thing too, right before they made it to him the boy passed out again. Kyle caught him and they quickly took him back to the exam room.

Mariam had stopped Rena and was asking her some questions about visions or something, that wasn't Gemma's concern. "Lay him on his side, I want to see that head wound first." Kyle did as he was told, and Gemma got to work on the wound. It wasn't too bad, but she used some of the glue to close it up. The wound was right behind his ear and beneath his hairline. "All right, gently roll him to his back."

Gemma checked his vitals and did everything she could. "He seems to simply be unconscious, but everything checks out otherwise."

From the doorway Rena spoke. "That happened before too, I was really concerned about his head more than anything else. And I'm glad none of us got sucked into whatever vision he's having right now. Because apparently that's a thing."

Gemma looked at the girl and raised her eyebrows. "This must be a new experience for you."

Rena let out a mirthless laugh. "Ya, but fate knows her shit. We all decided it was a gift and we'd figure out how to deal."

Gemma smiled. "Makes sense. And that is a very mature response from someone your age. I don't think I would have handled this with such aplomb when I was your age."

"I'll hang out with him here. You guys go have your meeting; can you give this to Mariam for me? I completely forgot when we were talking." She passed a tablet over to Gemma.

Gemma nodded. "Thanks."

Kyle and Gemma left Jesse in the care of Rena and went back to the living room with the others. "Do we want to start or wait for them to come out?"

Mariam responded. "We can go ahead and start, no way to know how long this vision will keep him under."

Gemma nodded and passed the tablet to Mariam. "I was told to give this to you."

Mariam opened it up and read through whatever was on it. "Interesting." She set the tablet down and looked around the room. "According to Jesse there was another one here. He was called away or something. But he watched you all around the fire yesterday. According to this he is already gone. I don't like that anyone who wanted to kill you all made it out. In addition, it seems like they are being controlled by some sort of magic. We are going to need to try to find out more." Mariam sighed. "It's never easy. Nothing is ever easy."

~

They finished talking, it didn't take long. Mostly Mariam wanted to double check that all of them were on the same page when it came to information sharing with the Kettle. "I think they're trustworthy Alpha," Bryce spoke up. "Yesterday we all took the time to go over the concerns and fears that both wolves and hawks had. When we did that, we got everyone together for a marshmallow roast. It was nice, seeing both packs, uh, kettle and pack, getting along and becoming friends. It's still a very new friendship but I think it's a good thing. The healer is pleased to have Gemma here and from what I understand Tabitha too, Gemma is going to train her to be a … what was it called?" He looked over at Gemma.

"Doula." Gemma smiled. "It was what she wanted to do before and I think if I had someone willing to help me make the rounds on the pregnant women that I would have much more time for our continuing research, not to mention the patients that need care for regular things like broken arms or checkups. The hawks have a healer, but she relies almost entirely on holistic medicine, she's been sending all the major cases all the way to the closest hospital, which is more than an hour drive, and just hoping nobody there would notice anything odd about the patients. She also confided in me that she's wanted to retire for over ten years but there was no one left to take her place. So, point being, I know they are grateful to have us here."

Daniel spoke up then. "The hawk Elders are also very excited to meet Jesse, when he's able obviously, they all go by different titles, but much like our elders they collaborate, and each have a specific focus of interest. The historian is very, very interested in the information Jesse might have found; he also thinks that it would be amazing for us to share our libraries. Which includes a lot of family bibles and some documents that are so old that they're scrolls."

Mariam nodded her head. "Unless anyone has any objections or concerns, I think that it is time for Hidden Pack to make our first alliance. With the hawks."

There were nods all around and some mumbled words in the affirmative.

"Good, then let's head over and meet with the hawk Alpha and Elders and get this alliance solidified." She smiled at the room.

The group made their way over to the lodge and walked in to find the hawk Alpha and his mate as well as four older hawks and three very young ones.

"I hope this is alright," the Alpha started. "In addition to the Elders I brought along Josh, Eunice and Kat. They will be taking over for Chuck, Will, and Gladys one day, we are still waiting for the fourth member."

"Aren't they a little young to be considered elders?" Daniel asked.

The Alpha chuckled. "Well, we consider the word to be about more than just age, it's a level of wisdom and council, and it's a type of calling. Our current Elders are just about ready to retire, we're just waiting on our fourth. Then these birds can go on some cruises and take much needed vacations."

Daniel nodded his head. "I like that. I know plenty of wise young people and plenty of old idiots. Your way makes sense. I'm guessing you would consider Jesse to be an Elder if he were in your kettle. He's feeling a little off right now, but I hope he'll be able to make his way over later."

As if the words summoned him, the door opened and in walked Jesse, leaning heavily on his mate.

"Sorry I'm late. That one took it out of me." Rena led him over to a table and had him sit next to Ben. Rena sat down the tablet and sketchpad and pencil pouch she'd been carrying under her arm on the table before sitting herself down next to Jesse. Daniel could see the worry etched into his sister's young features.

Something about that look made him ponder the way he'd been thinking of their mating. He agreed they were young. But how much of his opinions and those of his parents and brothers were simply based on society's constructs of when it was acceptable to be in a relationship? Had they all forgotten that fate, their wolf gods and goddesses, were the ones that made these decisions, and that they didn't make mistakes? Kyle was only six or seven years older than his sisters. He needed to think about this later though, he realized he hadn't heard the last couple minutes of talking. And the group was looking to him now expecting an answer. Deciding on honesty, he sighed. "I wasn't listening, I'm sorry, I got distracted about something. Can you repeat the question?"

Mariam laughed and Adam sighed. Adam was used to the way Daniel's brain worked. Mariam spoke up. "We were asking if you'd be able to fly Jesse back and forth every couple of weeks so we can get all of the kettle's text scanned in and make a mutual, shared database. He'll need to bring a few boxes of books and scrolls at a time and then return them when he's finished with that batch."

Daniel nodded. "Would it be more effective to set up a

second computer station for him here? Shared server. I could still fly him back and forth, but he could stay a few days at a time. That way he could do as many or as few as he could in that time frame without removing them from the kettle. They are probably as protective about their old texts as we are about ours."

"He's not wrong about that." The Alpha spoke. "I can see the Elders twitching from here. But if the only way for us to merge all of our information is for the young man to take it home to Oregon, then we'd allow it. But it would be more convenient to us if he was able to do that work here."

Rena and Jesse seemed to be deep into each other's eyes, almost as if they were communicating. Daniel was starting to wonder how strong their mating bond was, even without the physical act. That made him wonder if the physical act of mating was as important as they were always led to believe. Or maybe that was something that had been adapted and warped over time as well.

"I'll be coming with him when he comes over. I think two weeks here then two weeks in Oregon would work. Sometimes we all might want to come, or at least one or two additional… Would that work Mariam? Daniel?"

Mariam shrugged. "I think it sounds like a good plan. Would the cabin you're in now be sufficient for that? We would need to find somewhere for Rena to sleep too."

"Nope. I'm sleeping in the same cabin. There are two beds. And a couch. Until his visions are more under control, we are not leaving him alone. We've all decided that already. We won't break our promises to mom and dad and Judy, but no more being apart or alone. It's just not safe. Even if all five of us are here, me and Argie would just share one bed and the boys can flip a coin for the couch."

Daniel could tell she'd made up her mind and he hoped that Mariam wouldn't argue with her about it.

Mariam nodded her head. "All right. But I'm trusting you to keep your word."

Jesse laughed bitterly. "Don't worry. I can't even hold hands yet. I'm sure there aren't going to be any problems. And we all meant it when we promised the parents. So, no worries."

Josh looked like he was about to ask a question but before he could one of the older gentlemen put a hand on his shoulder and shook his head no. Josh scrunched his brow in confusion but let it go.

Mariam continued. "We will get you something set up here tomorrow to get things started for you. We'll have to drive into the big town to get what we need but it'll do. Are you ready to stay for a little while now? Or do you want to go back home and then come back in the next couple of weeks sometime to start."

Daniel laughed at Jesse's response. "I'm ready to stay. I brought enough for a while, enough to leave some here and not have to worry about toting clothes back and forth. Argie, Chris and Mickey should be here in a week or so, they're bringing more of our stuff too."

Mariam rolled her eyes. "Being the Alpha for a psychic can be annoying."

The group dinner and fireside chat was nice. Calm. No drama or incidents and it gave Kyle a lot of hope about what their future here would be like. He watched while the pups and the kids from the kettle ran around playing a game of freeze tag. They were having a blast. The teenagers had wandered off and were playing a game of sardines. Everyone else had split into groups, he could see everyone talking and laughing and he loved it.

Bea had insisted on coming out and enjoying the night with everyone else. Tabitha had enlisted some help from a few of her friends in the pack and they managed to set up one of the older couches that was supposed to be destined for the thrift store and brought it over near the fire. She also brought out a few quilts. They had wrapped the pups all together against Bea's chest with one of those baby wrap things. Tabitha had carefully sat herself on one end of the couch and insisted that Bea lay down with her head on Tabitha's small lap. From what he could tell his sister was talking to Tabitha's belly. He was glad they had finally come out to him and everyone else. He could see their love glowing around them. He couldn't imagine how hard it must have been to keep that a secret.

He found himself sitting on a small bench with Gemma nestled up to the side of him, comfortable under his arm, while Daniel sat on the soft grass between Kyle's legs, with his head leaned back on Kyle's thigh. While Kyle and Gemma were content to sit quietly and people watch, Daniel was telling stories and laughing with Josh from the kettle. It was a good thing that none of them seemed the jealous type because both Josh and Daniel had the type of personality that was just naturally flirty. They bantered back and forth for quite a while, making small talk and occasionally telling jokes that made all of them laugh.

As the sky grew darker and stars started to twinkle into night a little boy, about five or six if Daniel had to guess, came over and climbed up onto Josh's lap. Until then Kyle had forgotten that Josh had mentioned having a son when they all spoke yesterday. For the first time Kyle spoke up. "This must be Dylan. He looks so much like you. Except for that beautiful head of blond curls."

Josh smiled. "Ya, he got those from his mom. She had the most beautiful hair. She had never cut it, just trimmed it occasionally, it fell all the way down to the middle of her thighs. It was the only thing she was even a little vain about. For good reason."

Kyle wasn't sure if he should ask but chose to anyway. "How did you lose her?"

Josh shrugged his shoulders before sighing and then speaking. "She was strong, especially in hawk form, she was one of the sentries. One evening she was making a final loop around the kettle lands and was shot with an arrow. We still don't know who did it, and I doubt we ever will. We haven't had many problems with that kind of thing over the years. In fact, her death was the only poaching death we've had in my lifetime. I think the last was way back in the 40's or something."

"I'm so sorry you lost your mate. I can't imagine how painful that was for you." He tightened his shoulder around Gemma and reached his other hand down to hold Daniel's.

"She was my best friend and we loved each other plenty, but we weren't mates. She was clairvoyant, I'm not sure if you guys believe in that, but we do. And she was. She knew she was going to die before she met her mate, and she wanted a child. She asked and I couldn't imagine anything better than having a child with my best friend." The child in question had already fallen asleep in the arms of his father. "Later, when she was pregnant, she had dreams almost every night. In one she told me that I would find my mate within a haven. But that wouldn't be an easy conquest. Ever since you guys got here it's been on my mind. I haven't felt anything yet, but because of her, I am keeping an open mind."

Daniel sighed. "You are still strong and I'm sorry you had to lose your friend." I'm pretty sure there is going to be plenty more traffic here over time. I heard Mariam saying that they wanted to build a handful more cabins and make sure to get a stronger security detail here. Strong shifters to protect the ones that need it. I don't know if you're aware but Alpha Mariam saves people. She's part of a network that started even before the Hidden Pack was formed. It runs a lot smoother now and it has grown a lot bigger. Point of my story is that any number of women might be coming through here."

Josh smiled. "Doesn't have to be a woman. I just want to find my person."

They talked a while longer, enjoying getting to know Josh. Kyle had a feeling he was going to be a good friend to them. Slowly people were starting to pack up into cars and starting to leave, others from the pack making their way to their cabins. He knew it was time to go in too, he could smell, and through their mating link feel, that Gemma and Daniel were ready and eager to go in and go to bed.

Josh seemed to notice the looks between Gemma and Daniel. "I'm going to head off. I am so glad to have met you. If you need anything you can always find me at the diner. I'm one of the cooks there. It's our family that runs it. Beppie is my youngest sister. Thank you so much for the company. I'm going to get Dylan home and hope that he stays asleep the whole way. Have a great night."

They said their farewells and waved at others further away before Kyle spoke. "Come on. I need to get you two in the house before you combust."

"I don't know what's going on. I'm feeling odd. Almost like I have a fever. It started yesterday but it's even worse now. I just really need you, Daniel." She made a face after saying that. "I'm not making you feel left out, am I?"

"Not at all. You're respecting who I am. I know that if I wanted to join in, you'd welcome it. It's nice to know that you're not expecting it even after I told you how I feel. And I don't know about your feline side, but we had our wolves at each other which is totally normal when you find your mate. Or mates as the case may be. Maybe you're getting a double dose because of your cat. That's a guess."

She shrugged. "Maybe, and I'm sure I'll want to research that more later and I'll find it all very intriguing, but for now I just need to go to bed. I need, I need so much."

Daniel jumped up from where he had been sitting on the grass and held a handout to each of them. Kyle smiled and led the trio back home.

The bed loomed behind her, and she dragged her men towards it, she had taken one of their hands in each of hers as soon as they were up the stairs. She didn't release them until she came to the edge of the bed. She stripped. Fast and with a frantic need. Turning she saw that both of them stood there staring, still covered and inaccessible. "Why are you still dressed?"

Both men smiled at her and began taking off their clothes. They worked quickly seeing the state she was in. Finally, with a frown, Kyle spoke. "I think we should hurry, it's like she's in physical pain, I can feel it, can't you?"

Daniel nodded. "Yes."

The two quickly got on the bed on either side of Gemma who was kneeling in the center of the bed, her head resting on one forearm while her other hand was already between her legs, fingers sliding in and out of her pussy. She was making the most intriguing noises, desperate and sexy.

Kyle reached up one hand and started stroking a long line from neck to ass. "We have you; Daniel is going to make you feel so good." Daniel, who understood that was as much an instruction for him as a reassurance for her, quickly knelt behind their gorgeous mate.

"Are you ready Gemma? Or should we play for a while?" Kyle understood that Daniel was asking the question out of concern. Neither of them wanted to hurt her, but she was begging with her mumbled words and her body. She didn't even answer the question Daniel had asked her.

"Gemma," Kyle reached down and gave her cheek a small kiss. "Daniel is going to fuck you now alright? I know how important consent is, please tell him it's ok. I don't want you to suffer any longer."

It seemed as though his words cut through her fog at least a little. She let out a sound that would best be described as a chuff before grumbling under her breath. "Please, fuck me mate, please…"

Daniel didn't wait any longer. Kyle couldn't blame him. If he was feeling the connection as strongly as Kyle was, then Daniel understood that her need was almost a physical pain, she was in misery. Daniel lined himself up and entered her in one swift, deep, thrust. The feeling that came through their mating bond had Kyle moaning and Daniel reaching down to grab the root of his cock. "Oh fuck. I don't want to come yet. Gemma you are so tight right now. Even more than before. I don't know how long I can hold out. It's like I can feel everything you're feeling through our bond. It's almost too much." Gemma was beyond talking at this point.

Daniel finally seemed to get himself under control and

started making love to Gemma, slow and steady and deep. Whenever he bottomed out inside of her Gemma would make the sweetest sounds. Kyle was so happy that he was here and part of this. He felt like this was very important somehow. He leaned in and took Gemma's mouth in a kiss that seemed to go on forever. He loved this. The kissing, the small touches he was petting across her back, her sounds of need and happiness as he and Daniel made love to her. He kept kissing her and moved his hand to join hers where it played with her clit. She was so wet. He felt so right being in bed with them, touching them.

Kyle's fingers slid over her clit, faster and faster, sliding down and feeling the slide of Daniel's cock pistoning in and out. She was making the most desperate noises as he rolled her clit between his fingers. Daniel suddenly slowed himself down again. Kyle could see him squeezing his eyes closed in concentration. He slid his hand down and began to lightly massage Daniel's balls.

Kyle smiled when Daniel let out a squeak and then started slamming himself into their mate at a breakneck speed. "Gemma, please, come soon, I can't hold on..."

She needed something, Daniel could feel her need and frustration through their link, he just didn't know what she needed from them.

Suddenly, he had clarity, knew exactly what she was looking for. He wasn't sure if the thought came through their link, or if he was remembering something he'd heard before, or if it was just intuition, but he knew. He slid his mouth off of hers and licked a trail from her mouth to her earlobe which he sucked and nibbled on for a moment. He knew Daniel was about to lose his fight with sanity, so he licked and sucked down to that tender spot just between shoulder and neck, right below her ear, and bit. He bit hard, tasting the metallic tang of blood in his mouth he realized he'd broken skin, he was about to recoil and apologize but before he could do either Gemma screamed.

She screamed and then howled and neither sound was completely human. He could see all the muscles of her body clench tightly and even if they hadn't had a mating bond, he would've known that she was in the midst of an amazing orgasm.

Behind her Daniel let out a shout and pressed himself as deeply as he could inside of her. His body was shaking and the look of bliss on his face was beautiful.

Kyle couldn't believe how lucky he was to have two such amazing mates.

The pair of them slowly came down from their highs, Daniel sliding out of Gemma and collapsing on the bed next to her.

Kyle let go of her neck and lightly licked over the marks he'd left on her neck. He could feel himself blushing when he saw the bite and bruise that he'd left on Gemma. Before he could even think about apologizing or hiding Gemma spoke.

"Thank you. Both of you. I didn't know I would have such feline tendencies; I wasn't prepared and I'm sorry I didn't know to tell you guys." She yawned and stretched herself out on her side, facing Kyle. Daniel scooted his body close to hers and wrapped his arm around her.

Gemma snuggled into him but was looking at Kyle. "You look like you could use a little relief too."

Kyle was confused for a beat, then understood she was

referencing his erection. "I'm fine. That was wonderful. Holding you guys while you made love. It was perfect."

Gemma frowned but didn't argue. "So even though you're hard, you don't want to?"

Kyle smiled and gave a shrug. He was so grateful to have mates that cared enough to try to understand him and learn about what he wanted and needed. "No. If you still felt needy, I would gladly make love to you, but I'm satisfied with what already happened. My erection is a physical thing that I don't need to be a slave to. I love and enjoy being inside of you, and loving you, but kissing you and holding you are what I crave."

She smiled and squeezed Daniel's arm that was wrapped around her. "I think I'm starting to understand. Will you come a little closer and hold us?"

"Always."

*D*aniel still felt like he needed a few more hours of sleep when his alarm started blaring, but he had promised that he'd work with Jesse, getting every-thing set up with the computer that apparently was already at the post office in town. Mariam didn't mess around.

He might need to talk to her about finding a job for him within the pack. He was mated to one of the most important members of their little community.

He wondered if Kyle was feeling as useless as he was. He didn't even know what Kyle wanted to do with his life before they all met. Maybe they should both talk to Mariam.

Daniel showered quickly and got dressed in one of the three sets of clothes he had with him. He really needed to get his things here from Oregon. He made his way to the kitchen and started a pot of coffee. Before he could doubt himself, he picked up the phone and made the call to his sister's cell. He thought it was about to go to voicemail when it was finally answered by a timid voice not belonging to his sister. He knew Christian long enough to recognize him. Before he could ask why he was answering his sister's phone he heard the sound of someone being very sick, followed by a mumbled "never having sex again. If you come near me naked, I'm gonna rip it off…" and more gagging.

"Sorry to bother you, is she like this a lot?"

"Um. Couple of hours each day. Started last week. We are hoping it stops soon." Poor Chris. He didn't handle stress well. From what Daniel understood from talking to Elkan, Chris might be an Alpha, but he was a very needy sub that didn't handle stress well. He left that to his Beta mate Mickey, who he called Alpha when no one was looking, or when he was comfortable in his surroundings. Taking that into account he made the decision to not add any more stress or decisions to Chris' plate.

"Can I talk to Mickey since Argie is unavailable?"

There was a sigh of relief that made Daniel feel for the young man. Just answering the phone had caused him distress. "Yes, I'll get him."

There was movement on the other end of the phone and after a moment Mickey's voice came over the line. "Hey Daniel, what's up?"

Daniel wasn't surprised to hear so much authority in the teen's voice. He was suddenly handling a lot and had really stepped up to the plate. Elkan had bragged about how much he'd learned in just a couple of sessions.

"I was hoping you guys wouldn't be opposed to making a little extra money. I know you all helped get my brother all packed up and shipped and I'm hoping you'll do the same for me. I don't have as much stuff as

Elkan does. In fact, it's just a two bedroom apartment and I don't even have anything in the second bedroom. Never got around to putting my office together. Nothing for me to be too embarrassed about you guys seeing."

Mickey laughed. "Don't worry, we won't be embarrassed. Don't forget we've managed a couple visits with your brother. He broke our embarrassment button pretty fast."

Daniel smiled and poured himself some coffee. "I am nothing like him. Well, at least I don't have the embarrassing room he did. The only stuff that might embarrass me is in a lock box under the bed and you can just shove it in a box with the rest of my bedroom stuff. No big deal. To be honest there are only a few things I want from the kitchen and living room too, I'll make a list. Everything else you guys can either donate or keep for the duplex, I know it's only mildly furnished on one side and that you were going to have to buy a lot. So hopefully some couches and pans will help you out."

"Sounds great. We would be happy to."

"Shouldn't you ask Christian and maybe Jesse first?"

He chuckled again. "Jesse is going to be there for at least two weeks. Rena is staying with them the entire time. She told us before they left. We'll be done before then. Chris doesn't want me to ask. Argie will most likely just help us pack up the kitchen and maybe throw your clothes into some boxes. She isn't allowed to do any heavy lifting right now."

Daniel smiled. "Then we have a deal. I'll text you a list of the few kitchen and living room things I want to keep. Everything else will go on the truck. Tell me what day to have it there and I'll send movers. Unless you guys would prefer to use the company truck and drive it out to me."

"I'll talk to them about that and let you know today or tomorrow. I have to go. If your sister doesn't get some crackers and ginger ale in the next two minutes, I fear she'll kill Chris or myself."

"No problem. Good luck. Mom has a key to my place."

"Sounds good. Talk soon."

With that they ended the call and he decided he couldn't postpone the day any longer. He drained the last of his coffee and rinsed the mug. He quietly left and made his way towards the cabin that Jesse and Rena were staying in.

~

He knocked on the door and waited. When no one answered he carefully opened the door and peeked inside. No wonder, Jesse was still asleep on the bed and Daniel could hear the shower going, Rena must've woken up first and decided to let Jesse sleep while she got ready. He didn't want to interrupt his sister in the shower, but they really needed to get going. He made his way to the bed with Jesse in it, noting that both sides had been used and the other bed hadn't been slept in, and deciding quickly that that was above his pay grade. He heard the water turn off in the restroom but didn't feel the need to bother his sister. Jesse was sleeping on his stomach, Daniel reached down a hand and lightly tapped him on the shoulder, quietly saying his name. He was not prepared for the immediate and drastic reaction.

Jesse screamed. Not a small, surprised sound but a full

bodied scream filled with fear and terror. Before he even knew what was happening Rena was racing out of the restroom with a robe only half on. Jesse had thrown himself from the bed and was now huddled on the opposite side from Daniel, between the two beds on the floor. He had folded himself as small as possible and was still making the kind of noises you never wanted to hear from a person. Rena carefully knelt in front of him. "Jesse, wake up. Wake up all the way sweetie. Jesse…"

She continued to speak softly to him while he slowly began to bring his world into focus. Rena finally reached out a hand and held it up to Jesse's cheek. Wiping away a stray tear that had broken free. "It's ok. It was just Daniel trying to wake you up. I should have set the alarm for you. I'm sorry."

He leaned his face into her hand until it was practically trapped between his cheek and shoulder. His breaths were almost at a normal level again. He let out a long sigh. "You shouldn't have to set an alarm because you're afraid of talking to me or touching me when I'm asleep."

"Don't be like that. If it was any of us who were struggling right now you would be the first one to go out of your way to make life easier for us. Don't take this away from us. Taking care of your mates is the most important thing we can do. If you don't let us take care of you, then you're taking away that gift from us." Her words were so much more mature than Daniel expected. He wasn't sure why, but he realized then that the entire family still viewed the girls as little children, when in fact they had grown beautifully and were almost legal adults.

Jesse nodded. "I understand what you're saying but it might take me a while to stop feeling guilty or like a burden." He turned his face into her hand and kissed her palm. "Thank you."

Jesse quickly stood up and looked toward Daniel. "Sorry I overslept. I'll be ready in ten minutes. I need a quick shower." He walked into the restroom without a backward glance.

"Don't ever wake him up. Don't ever come up behind him quietly. Don't ever reach toward him too quickly, even to pass the potatoes. He needs calm and he needs to know his surroundings." Rena's voice seemed to hold a little bit of anger.

Daniel made his way around the bed and gave his sister a hug. "I'm very sorry. It won't happen again. I promise. I will let the few people that will be working with him frequently know as well. We don't want Jesse to be afraid of the people that are supposed to be his friends." He felt the moment she let go of the anger and tension in her body.

"Are you going to tell on us for sleeping in the same bed?" She looked up at him with her big eyes.

"No. I think you made a promise, and you'll keep it. I think that Jesse needs to have that security and his wolf needs to get used to smelling you and the others in bed with him so there aren't as many problems like the ones we had this morning. Also, when the time comes that you are ready to have a more physical relationship with him, you will want his wolf to be comfortable with you in bed with him. It will help give him comfort and ease some of the worries you all must have."

"Wow. I wasn't expecting that. And I wasn't expecting you to understand that all five of us are connected. Hopefully six soon. We're still waiting on our other mate."

"Don't forget you see connections, I smell them. I don't know how to explain it other than I know that the scent of Jesse and you compliment Argie, Mickey and Chris. For years I have known that you two and Mickey and Chris were connected, but I could tell there would be more. Just thought it might have waited a couple more years. That would have been ideal."

"Not for the guys. They need us now. So does our other mate, but we can't figure out where he is just yet, just that he's in danger. We are hoping Jesse has another vision of him that might give us some clues."

Just then Jesse walked out of the restroom in his jeans, rubbing the water from his hair with his towel. "Hopefully. I brought a little of the tea Sandra made me, with her new instructions, and I think if I focus on him while I drink and while I'm falling asleep, that I might be able to direct my visions." He hung the towel on a wooden peg outside the restroom door. Then turning he looked at Rena. "Did you steal all my shirts again? I can't find a clean one."

She sighed. "Fine. I was going to wear it today, I guess I can wear my own clothes." She reached into a pile of clothes that sat on the couch and tossed over a gray V-neck t-shirt. Jesse was laughing.

"I promise I'll get more, and we can share. I just can't do it this week. I need to earn some money first." He was smiling at Rena.

"How long will you be gone today?"

Jesse looked up at Daniel for an answer.

"I think it'll take about an hour or so to get to the post office, grab our boxes, and make our way back. But I need him to help set up in the small office in the main lodge. The one next to Bryce's."

Rena smirked. "When you get back let me know. I want to help too. I'll come and help set up and help get the first few books the hawks brought over scanned in. They started with the most recent texts, so I don't have to worry about knowing how to handle ancient texts. These books are from only a few years ago. Even I won't screw that up."

Jesse smiled. "You are learning though. I didn't think I'd get lucky enough to find a mate that also liked looking through old books and texts."

This was news to Daniel. "I had no idea!"

Rena shrugged. "I have hidden my inner nerd by reading lots of anthropology magazines and such. Actually, read a lot about the cultures of the areas that we think wolf shifters originated from. A lot of interesting stuff about skin walkers or shapeshifters in the local ancient lore. Also, lots of origin stories of how shifters came to be. I've been considering going to a university to get a degree in cultural anthropology. Argie likes to learn more about the scientific side. Gene studies and such."

Daniel let out a small "huh" then turned to Rena. "Do you think fate puts us together with people that complement our needs and strengths?"

That thought hung in the air for a silent moment before Jesse stood up from the chair he'd been sitting in. "I'm ready." He made his way across the small room towards Rena. Daniel noticed the subtle way Jesse avoided him, making sure to keep his back from him. When he reached Rena, he leaned in and they hugged. A long true hug.

Daniel heard a whisper. "Are you sure you're ok?" From Rena, and saw Jesse nod his head almost too small to be noticed.

When they separated, he gave Rena the most chaste kiss ever and whispered. "Love you. I'll hurry."

—————

*D*aniel borrowed Kyle's car for the short trip into town. He really needed to get his stuff here. He might need to trade his car in for something with better traction though. These roads were going to be hell in the winter.

As they drove, an uncomfortable silence filled the car. Daniel wasn't sure what to say, but he knew he needed to apologize for what happened earlier.

"Hey, I'm sorry for earlier. I didn't mean to scare you or startle you awake. Was just trying to wake you up. It won't happen again. Seriously."

It took a moment for Jesse to answer but just before Daniel thought his comment was going to be ignored Jesse finally spoke. "It's fine. I know it wasn't malicious. I just have bad reactions now."

Daniel didn't ask anymore questions and Jesse took that as a sign to continue. "I was attacked. I know that for the most part it's private and Mariam didn't go around telling everyone, which I appreciate, but sometimes it's hard because I forget that people don't know that I'm a basket case now."

"Hey," Daniel started. "Don't call yourself that. I know that you are probably talking to Joey about all of this, and I'm positive that he would tell you that belittling yourself like that isn't constructive." Neither spoke again for a few minutes. Finally Daniel broke their still awkward silence. "I was stabbed, in college, for no reason. I probably could've defended myself without any problems but not without using speed that regular humans don't have. I had this split second of thinking about if I should accidentally reveal myself or if I should hope that it was a small enough wound for me to heal from. I chose to let her stab me." He shrugged. "It was right before spring break. I almost didn't go back."

"Why did she stab you?" Jesse's voice still seemed a little timid in the quiet car.

"There had been a bunch of sexual assaults on campus that were being done as some sort of joke. Not rapes, but things like running up and grabbing a girl's butt or boobs. Completely unacceptable behavior that the frats were doing and thinking it was hilarious. Well, this girl had been grabbed multiple times apparently and I was behind her walking and managed to bump into her... she react-ed." He shrugged again. "It gave me a bit of fear though. Nothing like what you went through I'm sure, but enough that I almost dropped out of college as a freshman and for a few years whenever someone made sudden moves near me I kinda would freak out. I went to therapy for a while. Did the whole thing. It worked. Wasn't easy, but I was lucky to have only one bad experience. My point is this. Don't give up on your therapy, and don't worry about always feeling this way. I think you're surrounded with people that understand you. And now even if I'm the one needing to wake you up, I'll just call."

Jesse nodded but kept his eyes outside on the scenery.

"I noticed that you guys shared a bed, don't worry I'm not going to rat you out to mom, I just wondered if that helps you? Is that why you shared a bed? Or did you just want to?"

"At first we just needed to be near each other. Joey says that my experience and probably my age combine to make it that we aren't just jumping into sex. He says that we will know when the time is right and there is no shame in waiting. But I feel a need to be close to them. It's the only way I can sleep."

Daniel nodded. "Gotcha."

"You're really not going to tell Doc V?"

"Nope, I'm a big brother who is watching his sister take care of her mate in the way he needs while simultaneously keeping a promise to mom. You guys don't need anyone trying to tattle on you. You're practically adults. Just 50 or 60 years ago you'd all be old enough to marry in most states. Still are in some. You guys have your shit handled. No need for me to get involved unless you guys ever ask me to."

~

When they pulled into town they had people waving and smiling at them. It gave Daniel a lot of hope and good feelings about their future as allies.

They made their way to the post office and pulled into a spot right in front.

"I have no idea how much stuff Mariam decided we needed today. Hopefully not more than a single carload."

They got out of the car and entered the small post office. "Hey guys!" Daniel wasn't sure the name of the young woman working the counter but just by her appearance would bet money she was related to Beppie. "I have 9 boxes for you. I left them right there." She pointed next to the door. "I'm working alone today and have no desire to lift those boxes any more than necessary."

Daniel smiled. "No problem. I brought help, we'll get them loaded and out of your way really quick."

Before he even finished talking Jesse was out the door with the first big box.

"Hey, what's his name?"

"Jesse, but he's already mated."

"Dang. I am hoping for some new blood around here. Especially since talking to the doc at the meeting. I didn't realize you could have a fated mate that was not your same shifter type. That's going to open a lot more doors for me."

Daniel smiled. "There are plenty of young unmated men up at the camp, and more to come through surely, this camp is going to get a bit bigger and be used for those who want to be in our pack and live in a pack-like environment."

"Good to know."

Jesse was already back in and grabbing another box. And bright red. He'd obviously heard what she'd said.

They quickly loaded up the boxes and were back in the car.

"Before we head back, I want to stop at the store. I need real half and half. Gemma and Kyle both like that flavored crap. It's killing me slowly. And hopefully there are some shirts and such. I wasn't planning on moving here. I showed up with 3 outfits. It sucks. Do you need anything?"

"I didn't bring any money with me."

"It's fine. You're family. Don't let my sisters tell you any different. All of us have equal share in the company. And those of us who add to it get that for ourselves. Like all of the helicopter services and mechanics is me. I get all those funds but have to manage it all myself too. Point of the story, your mate has money. I'm not worried about grabbing you some necessities or snacks, but even if I was, I would just make Rena pay me back. Mates take care of each other." Daniel smiled at Jesse.

They parked in front of an old timey looking general store and went in.

"Thank god." Daniel headed for a small area that had limited clothes. He grabbed a few pairs of sweatshirts and sweatpants, a pair of jeans and plain t-shirts in a variety of colors. Then a pair of novelty pajama pants with hawks all over them. He smiled over at Jesse. "These are fun. Kyle will think it's funny."

Jesse grabbed a set of sweatpants and the matching sweatshirt. He shrugged. "I didn't think it would already be this cold at night."

They walked up and down the few small aisles of food and grabbed some things. Daniel started grabbing the stuff that he noticed Jesse lingering on. Takis, a pack of cola, some quick cook Alfredo bowls. Some frozen dinners too. He guessed that someone that had such a hard time sleeping probably found himself snacking in the middle of the night. If he was guessing right, the small fridge in their cabin was empty. He grabbed some grape soda and other snacks he knew his sister liked too.

They paid for their goods and helped the elderly man at the register bag it all up in some reusable canvas bags that they bought. They brightly exclaimed "Hawk's Landing General Store… for all your needs."

They loaded up the bags, which was easier said than done, and poor Jesse ended up with the bag of sweats under his feet and another bag of shirts on his lap.

"Well, hopefully that will hold us over for a while. I hate that I had to borrow Kyle's car."

"Mates take care of each other." Jesse laughed when Daniel made a face at his words being thrown back at him.

"Laugh it up smart ass… I'll remember."

Jesse seemed to enjoy his trip into town with Daniel. It started a little awkward, but they figured out how to be at ease with each other pretty quickly. When they were almost back, he finally spoke up. "Don't think I didn't notice you shoving stuff in the bags for me."

"I'm sure I have no idea what you're talking about." Daniel couldn't even keep a straight face while he said it.

They were still chuckling when they got out of the car.

"What's so funny?" Rena asked from her spot on the porch of the clinic.

For some reason that set them off again, soon all of their mates were looking at them like they might be insane.

Jesse was putting away the last of the groceries that he'd been gifted by Daniel. He had a couple more full bags of clothing items. In addition to the sweats he had picked out, Daniel had added a bunch of soft t-shirts and even a couple more pairs of sweats. That man was sneaky. Rena seemed glad though. She was already eyeing the t-shirts.

"So, I need to head over to the office. Daniel and Josh started putting it all together. Daniel's building the desk and Josh is going to do all the computer hook up stuff. Apparently, he does IT for a major company. So, he knows his stuff. I'm not an idiot, but I'm not going to turn down professional help. Apparently, Mariam got all the high end stuff for us, like super professional level. Hopefully the instruction manual will be easy to understand for the scanner/printer combo thing. It's huge and has so many buttons. It's like one you'd see in a print shop. It even collates. Once we have Wi-Fi it'll all connect to a main server back in Oregon. Felix is putting together the same stuff for me there in the smaller third bedroom of the duplex, the one Elkan used as an office. His desk was left so I don't have to worry about that." He paused and looked over his shoulder at Rena. "Is your parents' house or the duplex on official pack lands?"

She shook her head. Not phased at all by his sudden change of topic. "Nah. Our family is the only one there and dad has been running his Elder operations primarily out of the office for the last ten years or so. All of them get together once or twice a month but now that telecommuting is a thing, they are able to do most of their work from home. So officially, our city is considered almost Elder land, because there was no pack there and now everyone uses dad's address, PO Box in town, for official Elder stuff. So, Elder land. Why?"

He shrugged. "I feel like your family is all becoming members of the Hidden Pack, just wondered why it wasn't a problem for their previous pack, but basically all of you were just a pack with each other as Redfoots?"

"Ya, but some of us are stronger alphas than others and it's caused problems, even within the family. Mostly Adam and Elkan. Daniel is technically an alpha but he's not a super strong one. Sometimes people think he's beta. All the other brothers are betas. Felix is often mistaken for alpha though. He's actually almost more alpha than Daniel. It's weird."

"And you and Argie are both alphas."

"I guess. It's only since we met Mariam that we even considered that. My mother has always believed that females could be alphas, I think dad did too, but the official word was nope. So, we kinda assumed we were just bossy betas. Mariam says she sees red in our eyes."

"Interesting." He leaned back against their small counter. "Did you know that not all people can see the flash of red in an alpha's eyes? According to the old text it was a gift bestowed by the wolf gods to those that were worthy to lead so that they could pick the strongest members for their packs."

"But wouldn't that make too many fights? That many alphas in one pack?" She leaned against the small counter next to him.

"No, apparently the same people that can see the red can also detect gifted wolves. And packs with gifted wolves usually have one called an omega that can calm down the entire pack. There was an entire chapter on it, but I've only managed to translate and transcribe the very beginning of it. It was the book I was telling you guys about before. It has six different types of wolves listed. Not just the alphas and betas like we've been taught for years."

"I love that your nerdy little face lights up when you are talking about your books. It's super cute."

Jesse laughed. Full bodied. He actually had to wipe tears from his eyes. "I've never been told my nerdiness is cute. Before it was always treated like a disease that the pretty people acted like they'd catch if they hung out with me too long. And you are definitely pretty people." He blushed when he said that. "Thanks for making me laugh. That was the best laugh I've had for weeks."

*J*esse and Rena held hands while they made their way to the lodge. She said she wanted to see where he'd be working before heading over to the clinic to help however, she could and call and check in with her mom and Argie and the guys.

"This is nice!" Rena said the words way louder than necessary and before Jesse could ask her why she did that he heard a loud thump from under his desk and some mumbled curse words. Her smile was wicked, and he had no doubt the volume of her previous statement had the exact reaction she was looking for.

"I'm just finishing up with the little caps over the screws and stuff. Then Josh will get your monitors and keyboard up here." Daniel was still rubbing the top of his head.

From the opposite side of the room came a chuckle from Josh. "How's your head?"

"Not a word."

Rena laughed at her brother's response. "How many times has he brained himself?"

"At least five." He smiled at them both. "I just finished programming this. The only thing left to do is add the Wi-Fi information and sync it up when we finally get that up and running. It'll work right now and save to the computer, I hardwired it so don't trip, that'll go away once we have the Wi-Fi. It'll all be wireless. Your Alpha sent a couple of very impressive exterior hard drives for you to take back and forth until we get it all working right."

Josh made his way over and carefully placed the monitors on the desk. "The keyboard and mouse are Bluetooth, so you don't need to worry about extra cords." He reached down and grabbed them, placing them in front of the monitor.

"I'm going to head over and call mom and the mates. I'll bring some snacks later." She gave him a small hug and left.

"You two are adorable." Josh seemed to have a bit of longing in his voice.

"Ha! Two." Daniel laughed while brushing the dust off of his pants.

Jesse must've felt more comfortable than he realized. "This from the guy with an extra mate too?" He realized he'd poked fun and wasn't sure what the reaction might be. But he could feel his face reddening. He only relaxed when Daniel started laughing.

"Got me there. Not to mention Adam." He rubbed his head again. "Do you think it's weird that four out of seven siblings all have more than a single mate? So far anyhow. Gideon isn't mated yet." He looked from Josh to Jesse and shrugged. "I think it's odd."

"I don't know. There was a partial scroll I found at the old pack. I wrote down as much as I could. Basically, it said that packs that are in good favor with the fates or gods or whatever get more fated mates in general and then it started to say something about additional mates but the rest was cut off. I would think that the fact that it was all together might indicate that a worthy pack might just get that as a perk."

They were silent for a couple minutes. Finally, Josh spoke. "Then I hope our alliance puts me in good favor with the gods and fates too. I have been wanting my mate and wouldn't mind more than one. Just finding my special one would be nice too though."

They talked a little more before Josh finally took a little time to explain the basics of the scanner and where to find the links to the different programs he'd installed. Finally, just when he thought his brain would explode, his mate and Daniel's saved him.

"We brought snacks." Kyle was standing in the doorway holding a couple of filled plates. "You should come out here and we'll sit and snack and then you can come back in and get started on work when we're done."

Josh said he had to take off, but Jesse noticed the longing in his eyes when he saw Kyle reach over and give a small kiss to Daniel's cheek. He hoped Josh found his mate soon. Maybe he'd try his meditation before bed to see if he could focus on Josh. It was something Joey had recommended to see if he could somehow, at least some of the time, control his visions instead of the other way around.

The four of them chatted and ate. He knew it was Rena's doing but their snack was a bunch of cut up fruit and veg, some cheeses and some cold cuts. It was her standard snack. She loved to make plates like this at home too.

When they were done, they left Jesse alone with his new office. That's when it really hit him. He had an office. And a second one back in Oregon. He had a job that the Elders were paying him for. He still wanted to finish school and maybe get a degree in library sciences, but for now, he was contributing to the family. Their little family was young and even though they hadn't mentioned it to the parents, they were all worried about how they were going to take care of not just themselves but the twins that were coming soon, mostly because of their age. He suddenly felt proud of himself and as if maybe, just maybe, he wasn't going to be a burden to his family or new pack.

He was smiling when he made his way to Bryce's door and gave a small knock even though it was open. "Sorry to bother you, but the Elder said I could find the first stack of books in here?"

Bryce looked up with a smile on his face. "You're all ready to get started? That's great. You are really helping to bridge our pack with their kettle, and hopefully save some of these old documents before they degrade any more than they already have."

"That's the plan. I am hoping to find a lot of the old traditions and lore and folk tales. You can learn so much from a society and culture based on their stories."

Bryce made his way over to a small shelf and grabbed a stack of books. There were only four of them, but they were very large. "Apparently these are the newest family bibles from the kettle. He figured you'd want to work your way back."

"Thank you. This is amazing. I can't wait to start our database and get everything going. This is going to be great." He headed back to his office with a smile on his face and got to work.

Daniel wasn't sure how to have this conversation, but he still felt like it was necessary. He softly knocked on the cabin door because it seemed quiet, and he remembered what it was like when he accidentally woke up his siblings from naps. He did not want to be on Tabitha and Bea's list of people to hate.

Tabitha opened the door with a finger to her lips and a smile. In a hushed tone she spoke. "Hey Daniel. What's up?"

"Can I come in for a moment? Or you and Bea come out here if you're worried, I'll wake up the pups." He kept his voice hushed as well.

"You can come on in. They do fine as long as we don't have sudden noises. We'll just try to stay a little more quiet than usual."

She ushered him in and led him to the one chair they had next to the couch where she took a seat next to Bea who looked exhausted.

"I'm really sorry to bother you. But… well you know I helped identify the shifters by their species because I have a ridiculously good sense of smell?"

Both women nodded.

He took a deep breath and continued. "I'm not sure if you're aware, but not all of the pups are wolves. In fact, I think only one is a wolf and the other two will present as foxes. Actually, one of the girls, I think Tabbie, she smelled of both so don't be surprised if she is able to shift into both forms." He waited to see if he would get a negative reaction or hit or his abilities questioned, but none of that came. Instead, both women smiled.

"You don't have to be nervous. We knew ahead of time that he was a fox. So, we understood that the pups could be either. It was a risk we were willing to take."

"Good. I'm glad you're not upset. I didn't want to overstep but I was afraid you didn't know, and it would come up and startle you or something. I don't really know. I just wanted to make sure you knew."

"Thank you. We appreciate it. It's nice knowing that you cared enough about us to come and talk to us even though it made you uncomfortable. So ya, thank you." Bea seemed to be sincere, and Daniel was glad to see that there were no hard feelings or hurt ones.

Daniel smiled. "My family loves when any of the kids find a mate, or mates, because they consider it a gain. My Parents and siblings, and me of course, will consider you family by default. You just gained a lot of people that care about you two and your pups."

The women looked at each other before turning back to Daniel. "All three of us moved with Bryce knowing we would just have the three of us." Tabitha started. "Unlike Bea and Kyle, I had a father there. He just was not a very nice person. He's the only loss I suffered moving here. So, if I can say that I have managed to gain some family I'm coming out ahead. So, thank you again."

~

*D*aniel left their cabin and headed back towards the clinic. A large group of young men were busily cleaning gutters on both the rear of the clinic and all around the lodge. Near the edge of the forest right behind the lodge there was another group of people clearing some land, moving big rocks out of the way, and dragging a large fallen tree just a little into the shadows of the forest. He watched a few more minutes before he realized that they were clearing a garden space.

"This time of year they won't be able to plant a whole lot, but some of the fall vegetables should take hold." Bryce startled him a little.

"What's with the log?"

"Mushroom farm. We'll keep picking them all until they stop blooming. Any extra we dry and use for soup in the winter."

"Have you considered getting chickens or goats? They would both thrive here. Rabbits too. I saw a great coop plan that was also a pen for rabbits, like a two-story thing." Daniel asked.

"I just don't know if I have the manpower to get a coop up and ready in time, might have to wait until spring."

"If it's all right I'll look into it, see what style would be best for you and the weather here, and I'll get back to you with some plans. Even if we can't get it done this year, maybe I can help in the spring."

"That would be great." Bryce nodded. "We were clearing some of the fallen stuff in the rear of the camp and found a smoke house in pretty good shape and another small building that was probably a coop. It's messed up, maybe you could look at it and see if it's worth saving. We are going to have to get a lot of food stuffs and such for winter, might not be able to get down to the stores too often."

"Let Mariam know, she might arrange some bulk purchases if she knows it's going to be necessary."

They chatted for a few more minutes before Daniel made his way in to see how Jesse was doing. The boy in question was squinting at the computer. "… maybe sigma? I think it says sigma, maybe… damn it."

Daniel smiled at the young man's murmurs. "How is it going?"

Jesse didn't even flinch, he must have heard Daniel coming. "Good. I have scanned in the first two books that the hawk's let us borrow. I'll do the other few things tomorrow. I'm working on a manuscript from the wolf elders. It is in bad shape and I'm trying to add color filters to see if it makes me able to see different words or letters. It's really old. Talks about what I think says 'sigmas' but it's partial, a lot of the writing has degraded."

"I was just checking to see if there is anything you need. We are thinking about driving down to the diner for dinner tonight, wondering if maybe you and Rena wanted to come."

His face looked up finally. "Sounds good. How soon?"

"Probably thirty minutes or so."

"I will close down my programs and go get ready then. I'll let Rena know."

"Just head over to the clinic when you guys are ready."

*I*nstead of driving all in one car, Rena decided to drive the car she brought from Oregon. She needed to fill up the tank anyhow.

"So, we're just having dinner in town and then going straight back to the camp?" Rena asked.

Jesse shrugged. "I think so. I do want to give back the two books I already finished, but that should only take a minute. Then we are done."

She nodded her head. "How about we go to the little park and swing for a minute. I know it's usually a kid thing, but I love swinging. Then maybe grab some tea from the store. It was great of Daniel to grab me some stuff but, I want a kettle and tea."

"Sounds good to me. I even brought some of the modified mix Sandra made me. She said to dilute it with another tea, so that will work out great for me." He smiled as he looked over at her.

They parked at the diner and joined the other three inside.

Jesse and Rena were both enjoying the names of all the food items and all the fun decor in the small diner. When they first had walked in they saw that the others were seated in the last booth in the rear corner, it was a horseshoe booth, but Jesse noticed they had left the wall side completely free for him. He just knew it was Daniel doing what he could to help Jesse be comfortable.

They ordered dinner and just sat chatting. It was nice. Almost like a double date. For the first time in what seemed like forever, Jesse didn't doubt himself, he just put his hand down and carefully took Rena's into his.

It shouldn't have been a big deal.

Normal people do it all the time.

So why did he notice a tear in her eye? If that wasn't hard enough, he could hear that everyone at the table had gone quiet.

Before he felt obligated to break the silence or apologize or something equally as awkward the server came and started putting all the food at the table, asking if it looked good, if they needed hot sauce or ketchup, all of the normal stuff. By the time all of that was done the moment had passed. And instead of looking shocked, Rena just looked happy. Jesse was relieved to see that just that fast and for no reason he could put his finger on, he felt a little better.

They spent the evening enjoying the company and food and just relaxing. Jesse didn't realize how stressed out he'd become over the last few days. He hadn't felt it, it wasn't some big sudden thing. He had been collecting it like a snowball being rolled. He wasn't sure why, but he knew he should try to figure it out. Find what had been causing this feeling within him. But for right this moment he was feeling good.

They finished their meal and told the others they needed to stop at the store to grab some things, not to worry if they didn't see them for a while. After waving off the others they decided to leave their car where it was and walk around the little downtown area. It was basically a long block, not a great distance and Jesse was glad for the stroll. Joey had told him he always needed to be honest with those closest to him, especially his mates, if he wanted them to understand what he was going through and so they wouldn't accidentally make it worse.

"I'm having a hard time. The meal was nice and really seemed to help, but I feel pretty stressed out. I'm not sure why and I slacked on journaling the last couple days. I will start again when we go to bed tonight. I just wanted you to know. If I'm short with you or seem off, it's not you, and I know it's me, and I have no idea why, but I'm working on it."

Jesse hadn't even realized he'd been holding hands with Rena again until she gave him a little squeeze. "That's fine. You know that I will do my best to help you figure it all out too, right?" Jesse gave a small nod. "Good. I was worried that being outside of your new routine might upset you for a while. Sandra gave me some tea to help you calm down and meditate. Totally different from your other tea. She didn't recommend we mix them at the same time but as long as it's been a couple hours it should be fine to have the other. So maybe when we first get back, I'll make that for us, she recommended I have it too since I seem to get upset when my mates are upset. Then we will have plenty of time to calm down and relax a little before you use the other tea before bed. If you're still wanting to?"

"I am. I feel like something important is missing from my vision. More like I'm missing something. And I feel like time is running out. I don't know why. I am confident in my previous vision of us not meeting him for at least another year. But I feel like we are supposed to do something to help him even before that." Jesse let out a small growl. "It is so frustrating only getting glimpses and pieces of the important stuff, but sometimes I'll have a 2-hour cinematic piece of life of people I've never even met just having dinner at their house and talking about what they did at work that day. I wish whatever fate or god or goddess or trick of nature that gave me this ability would prioritize a little better."

Rena smiled. "I don't think it works that way, but I can see how that would be annoying. I'm sorry you can't close the tabs you don't need and use a search engine to get to what you want." They both laughed at the imagery.

Soon they walked into the small store and smiled at the woman behind the counter. It was nice. No hurry and no rush and no feeling embarrassed that someone else was paying. Well, less embarrassed.

"I should also tell you that I'm embarrassed by how much you and your family are paying for me. I'm trying not to be, because if I was well off, I'd have zero problems paying for any of my mate's needs and I'm trying to apply that same logic. But I don't know. I'm working on it." He looked away from her eyes, a bit of red in his cheeks.

"What? For starters, I'm glad you're working on it. But secondly, you have an official job, on top of starting classes to get your GED which is impressive. And the job comes with money. Did my dad not tell you how much you were making or what the plan was?"

Jesse scrunched his brow. Not really. "I get really nervous around your dad; he's a really strong Alpha and it makes me uncomfortable even though I know he's safe. Sometimes I blank out when he's talking to me. Same with Adam."

"Well, Chris and Mickey are working at the hangar again for a while in addition to the side jobs they are doing and their GED classes. They don't make as much as you but it's more than sufficient. Everything is direct deposit into your individual accounts. Just like my share of the family company profits. Then the amount we pay monthly is taken out of our accounts - split five ways equally. Once we find our other mate, we will reevaluate that. Then the rest is just there in your account."

"I have an account? How much am I getting paid?"

"Oh man, Dad really needed to make sure you knew what was going on, I'm not sure they realized just how out of it you were. you and your mom both have accounts that Tiny set up for you, I guess. There was a little starter money in there and when you're ready you can start paying pack dues, but Mariam said no rush. Gimme your phone."

He opened up his phone and handed it over. Rena made some quick swipes and clicks, and a banking app opened up on his phone. She showed him the deposit page.

Jesse's eyes popped. "That's how much I get paid every month?"

Rena laughed. "No. You work for the council of Elders. You are expected to be dedicated and work whenever they call. That was last week's paycheck. Your first check. You will have that deposited every week."

Jesse couldn't fathom it. "We have never had money like that. We weren't too broke, or poverty stricken but we still had nothing like this."

"Well, this is it. Your calling. You found it early. You are saving and translating and deciphering and even having visions about the histories and texts of our pack and all the wolves are lining up to be next on the list when the Elder's scrolls and books are done. Plus, then we let the hawk's cut in line so that we could more easily solidify our alliance, but that's fine. You have your entire life. Don't forget, you are the only person who has felt drawn to this or been able to make heads or tails of it for generations. The Elders are fully aware of how important you are. The salary wasn't even proposed by my dad, so don't let yourself think this is pity or favoritism. He excused himself from that part of your hiring process. The other's deliberated and decided this was your pay for now. It'll likely increase over the years."

They started walking again, grabbing a stove top kettle, and a toaster. "I can't believe there was no toaster. Let's see if they have a microwave here somewhere, if not I'll order one on the phone before we leave town and lose signal."

"What about the house? How much are we paying for that each?" Jesse was aware that Rena had thought this conversation was over and had moved on, but Jesse's brain was still processing.

She laughed. "Technically the house has belonged to the pack since it was built years and years ago. But then Elkan bought the entire duplex. He did that over 15 years ago. He isn't looking to make any profit on the house. He asked the same price which he paid, which was hardly anything at the time because the pack didn't try to make a profit either. So, we are paying hardly anything each. All the other stuff we want to do we will have to pay for and arrange who pays what and all that crap later. But for now. We are more than fine. So, help me find a microwave and then I want a cheesy tourist sweatshirt and some junk food and a salad and maybe some ice cream. I'm in a mood."

Jesse smiled. "Understood. And…. yes dear."

They wandered around the store for a while grabbing things that caught their eyes. For the first time in his life, he didn't worry about if they were spending too much on food to be able to make their electric bill.

"When we are all together next, I want to sit down and discuss this and all of our expenses. Things like the power bill, the gas bill, cell phone bills, that stuff."

Rena smiled at him. "No problem. We can totally do that."

They paid for their things and loaded them into the car. "Did you still want to go sit in the park?"

Rena thought about it for a moment before answering. "No. We can do that whenever. I want to get back and get that first batch of tea brewing. I think a quiet night in with our books and maybe working on the puzzle I bought sounds perfect."

"Sounds good."

They put on their favorite playlist and sang their way back to their cabin home.

They hopped in the car and waved goodbye to Rena and Jesse. He drove until he saw they weren't looking and then Daniel, who was in the back seat this time, grabbed his phone and made a call.

"Hello" Daniel smiled at his brother's voice. He missed his twin and needed to see him more. Sometimes growing up sucks.

"Hey, can you do me a favor and have Joey check in with Jesse? Give him a while to see if he calls first but if you don't hear from him tonight, call the main lodge number in the morning, he'll be there and has a phone in his office."

"Sure. What's going on?"

Daniel sighed. "I don't know. He has been getting more and more stressed the last couple of days. It was good tonight at dinner for a while but there were big moments of stress that bled through."

Daniel noticed his mates looking at him with

scrunched brows. He silently pointed to his nose and shrugged. They both smiled and nodded.

"I will tell Joey as soon as he's done with current appointment. I'm attempting to wait patiently. Tonight we're supposed to go downstairs."

Daniel laughed at his brother's excited tones. He sounded like a kid one Christmas. "Well, have fun and don't forget his cane."

"IT WAS ONE TIME!"

Daniel hung up with a laugh.

Gemma turned in her seat to look back at him. "So, you can smell emotions too?"

He nodded. "Strong ones at least. Stress, Pain, Desire..."

"Interesting. What else can your super nose do?" She smiled while she spoke. He loved her smile.

"I can smell certain illnesses in people. I know a lot of shifters can smell things like cancer or infection, but I seem to be able to smell them way before anyone else. I told a college hook up to go to the doctor. He smelled like cancer. He thought I was insane, but I must have scared him enough to go because it turns out he had breast cancer. Super rare in men and not something you usually check for. Especially in a healthy twenty-year-old athlete. It was super small, but they were able to get it all and he was fine. He never talked to me again, but whatever. I freaked him out."

They were silent for a while and then he continued. "My mom is a doctor. And a vet, technically. Sometimes when she knows something is wrong but can't find what it is, she will get the patient's permission for me to come in.

I've helped her multiple times. Had a woman with on again off again stomach pain that lasted for years but she struggled to decipher where the pain was coming from. I walked in and pointed directly to her appendix and said it was there. They did blood work, came back normal, did an ultrasound and it showed nothing. Finally, they decided to just remove it just in case. Turns out she had not a ruptured appendix but a small tear, it kept getting infected then her body would heal, then it would get infected all over again. Eventually it would've ruptured badly and maybe killed her, but it had been doing this infection then healing thing for like five years. Super weird."

Gemma cocked her head. "I've heard of that in a few humans. It wouldn't have occurred to me to check for that in a shifter."

Kyle made eye contact in the rearview mirror really quick. "Did you always have this ability?"

Daniel smiled. "The first time I remember realizing that my sense of smell was super strong was when I was like three or something. I woke up Elkan really late, or at least late for a toddler, we'd been sleeping, and told him to come downstairs with me for hot chocolate because I could smell mom making it. He didn't really want to, but his mate was down there, and he loved hanging out with him so he didn't fight me too hard. I got to drink his cup too, if I remember correctly, he fell asleep on Joey's lap."

"Wait, he knew Joey since he was three?" Gemma seemed confused.

"Actually, Joey was Adam and Ben's friend before we were even a thought. He realized when mom was preg- nant that one of us was his mate, he could feel it even then. But he never had any sort of creepy thoughts or inappropriate ones. I don't know at what age that would've changed. When we were maybe six or so Joey and his sister took off for safety reasons, they only met up again in the last couple of weeks actually. Fortunately, even though Elkan was really hurt by being abandoned he took time to understand what had happened and worked through it. It's still there, the pain, but they're getting better and stronger, it shouldn't be long before that's a completely forgiven thing. I hope. I was really mad at him for a long time too, I was the one that Elkan cried too, the one he told about all his pain. Twins do that. Well, at least we did."

From the front seat Kyle spoke up. "Bea and I were like that for a long time. It changed some when our parents died. I felt the need to take care of her, it was almost like I let my brother role become a parenting role. It's not the same thing I know, I wasn't really her parent, but it felt that big when I was younger. I was so grateful for Bryce. If it wasn't for him, who knows what would've happened to the Cacherbête kids." He smiled back at Daniel.

Daniel cocked his head to the side. "Embarrassing to admit but I didn't know your last name until just now. That's my mom's maiden name. Are you related to the Cacherbête pack?"

"Not by blood, no. Long story short, those folks owned my folks long ago, which meant when they became free men they took that name, and then even after slavery was a thing of the past they continued to act as if they owned us. My father grabbed mom and they took off. The Alpha over there is an asshole from everything my parents told me. Bryce took in my parents when they had nowhere to go. Then took in me and Bea when we had nothing left."

Daniel frowned. "Mom is his niece…" He saw a horrified look cross Kyle's face. "…don't worry, she escaped him too. That part of the family is distant and not particularly acknowledged. Just so you know, no one hates the Alpha Cacherbête more than Mariam. Seriously, no one."

He left it at that, it wasn't his story to tell.

"Snow" Gemma's word came out of nowhere and without context. Both men seemed confused. Finally, Gemma laughed. "Gemma Snow. That's me."

Kyle and Daniel both started laughing.

33

*J*esse had an office.

He was currently sitting in his chair and typing out some translations, no big deal, when he reached for his pen. It was out of ink, so he opened his drawer and grabbed another pen. He wasn't sure why, but something about that act of opening his drawer and grabbing a pen made him realize that he was sitting in his very own office. He struggled falling asleep last night, even with the tea, and thought about his new job and salary. He was only a teenager. It didn't seem like he deserved this. At least in his own head. He knew he was doing something important, but his own self-doubt was huge.

He was frozen looking at the screen, thinking about nothing and everything, when the phone rang.

"Hello?"

"Hey Jesse, it's Joey."

"Hey Joey, what's up?" Jesse reached for his bottle of water, carefully taking a sip.

"Not too much. Just wanted to call and check in. See how you're doing up there, new friends, new responsibilities, all of that?"

"Joey, you are the worst liar I've ever met. I'm guessing someone called and told you I was having a case of the wiggins. Probably my sweet mate or maybe my brother-in-law?" He smiled at Joey's sigh.

"I'm not saying who, but yes, I was asked to check up on you. So, tell me honestly, how are you doing?"

Jesse was glad that Joey didn't try to lie or cover up the truth with pretty words and subterfuge. He was still a little annoyed that someone ratted him out to Joey, but he'd deal with it. It wasn't like Jesse didn't realize that he needed help. It still feels like he was tattled on.

"I hate that they told on me, but I know it was needed. I know I need to come to terms with the fact that people are looking out for me."

"Why do you think that bothers you so much?" Joey asked the question with care.

Jesse sighed and thought for a moment before answering. "I've always been strong. I've always been the ones my friends came to when things were too much, and they needed help. I don't like this side of it. It feels so weak."

Joey made a small "uh huh" and Jesse could imagine him nodding his head. "It's ok to be the one that needs someone to lean on sometimes. In fact, it's normal. People change and evolve and have experiences. That's life." He paused for a moment and Jesse was glad that he didn't feel the need to fill the silence when he talked with Joey. "Let me ask you a question. What is the number one thing you need to do to be a good mate, or even a good pack mate?"

"Take care of your mate. Take care of your pack. We

always take care of each other, that's the purpose of a pack. You care for your mate, that's your number one responsibility, especially if you're lucky enough to find your fated mate. I guess it would be the same for a chosen mate, why don't we teach that?"

Joey chuckled. "That's an entirely different thing. We'll come back to it. So, let's talk about taking care of your mates. You know if Rena or even Argie, Chris or Mickey needed you, that you would be there in a flash to ease their burden."

"Of course."

"Then you need to realize that when you don't let them take care of you, or try to act like you don't need help, that you are actually robbing them of their right to take care of their mate too."

Jesse froze. He may have even forgotten to breathe for a moment. "I never thought of it that way. Even after listening to Rena try to explain it to me. It just didn't click until you said it just now."

"We have the bad habit of telling people what their responsibilities are but never accepting that it goes both ways. We need to get into the habit of letting people know that it's ok to ask for help. It's healthy to ask for it. We can't do it all on our own. Especially when something traumatic has happened."

"I hear what you're saying."

"Good. Is there anything else you want to ask me or talk about?"

Jesse thought about it for a minute. "I don't think so. Did Mariam or Daniel tell you about the attack?"

"They did."

"Good. I don't think we've seen the end of that. And I

don't think that it's going to be isolated to this area. I think they are everywhere."

"I will stay vigilant then. I'll tell Elkan what you said too. That way we can keep an eye out at the club as well. Thank you."

Jesse loved that no one in this pack ever doubted his visions or intuition. They valued it. "I'll talk to you in a couple days. I think I'll be alright until then. If I'm not, I will call. Promise."

"Talk to you later. Bye."

Jesse ended the call with a smile and was glad that he had someone to talk to. He was glad he had people looking out for him too.

~

Right before lunch one of the hawk Elders showed up with another stack of books.

"Hi Wil!" He stood and cleared a space on the desk for the books the older man was holding.

"I was fiddling around this morning with the books, and I think I want you to see this. I think you should do your scan stuff with it next." he stopped and looked up, finally making eye contact with Jesse. "Hello. Sorry. I'm just excited. I don't think this is the first time we've had an alliance!"

The two of them sat and started going through the books that Wil had brought over. They didn't realize how long they'd been working until there was a light knock on the door.

"You guys have to come eat. You skipped lunch. You

can't skip dinner too." Rena wasn't asking. Jesse smiled at her authoritative tone.

"Thank you mate. I didn't know we'd been in here this long. Thank you for taking care of me."

Rena blushed. "Well, you're welcome. Come eat. You too Mr. Wil."

The older gentleman smiled. "On our way. Now that you woke us up from our scholarly stupor, I can smell how good dinner is going to be."

They closed down the computer and stored the books in an order that only the two of them understood and left the office. Locking the door behind them. It was one of the only requests the hawks had, that their books always be locked up when Jesse wasn't actively using them. Jesse agreed. The texts he would be working with were priceless.

Dinner was loud and joyous. The entire pack was in the lodge sharing. Jesse sat down next to Rena when she patted the seat next to her. "Mr. Wil, I saved you the seat right here" she indicated the empty space directly across from Jesse.

"I think we need to talk to Bryce about what we've found. Maybe call the Alpha too. I know there is still more to translate and transcribe but we know enough." Jesse wasn't surprised that Wil made the recommendation. He was starting to realize just how welcoming the hawks were to the idea of an alliance and merging their knowledge.

"I think you're right." Jesse nodded. "After dinner we will find Bryce and see about calling Mariam and letting her know too."

A large pan of lasagna was placed in the center of the

table next to a big basket of garlic smelling biscuits and bowls of salad. Pitchers of water and what looked like iced tea were scattered on the tables as well.

From the front of the room Bryce stood up and spoke. "Thank you all for the hard work we've put in today. I know we have managed to get this place up and running in record time. We still have plenty to do before we can rest, but it's coming along so much faster than I thought it would. Thank you to our new friends that have been coming up and helping us out so much. We are grateful. Enjoy." he sat down and everyone started serving themselves.

Jesse looked around and just now noticed how many hawks were in the room with them. He also noticed that the large windows were sparkling clean and had curtains now. He wondered what outside looked like because a lot of the people in the room looked as if they'd been working hard for hours. He started to feel a little guilty for not helping.

"Stop it." Rena's voice broke into his ponderings.

"What?"

"You're feeling guilty for not helping out more with manual labor. Don't. Alpha gave you a job to do and you've been doing it."

Jesse smiled. "How did you know I was thinking that?"

Rena smiled back and reached down to hold his hand. "Because you're my mate. I know you."

Apparently, they were smiling at each other for a moment too long, because from across the table they heard Wil. "You two are so damn cute. And there's more of you?"

Jesse nodded his head and used his free hand to grab

his fork. "Yep. Eventually there will be six in total. For now, there's five."

They spoke a little about the different abilities that Jesse, Rena and Argie all had. How they thought more people had abilities than they realized and how they hoped to find a way to help people find their abilities.

It was a nice meal. Laughter, conversation, and good food. Jesse felt lucky to have found it.

~

After dinner Jesse made his way towards the front of the room where Bryce was talking to a little girl. "You are correct. There probably should be some sort of indoor playground or playhouse since it snows so much here. I will put it on my list of things we need to do. For now, until we can build it, what if we put some fun stuff on the far side of the room over there and you pups can come play whenever you want to. Does that sound like a good plan?" He waited patiently while the little girl had a make-believe conversation with the doll she was holding.

"Ok. We like that idea. Can we get a play kitchen? And monster trucks?"

"I will add them to my list right now." Bryce took out his phone and showed her the list he had, and he carefully typed 'play kitchen' 'monster trucks'. The girl smiled at him and skipped away.

"Hey gang, what can I help you with? Do you need something when I place the order tomorrow?" Bryce held up the phone with the very long list on it.

"I think we have everything we need. We actually

wanted to talk to you about something we found today in the books. Maybe we should ask Mariam to join in too, tell her at the same time." Jesse was trying his best to get over his fear of talking to alpha males. He thought he was doing pretty well. Bryce made it easy, he was a really nice guy.

"Let's go to my office then. I moved a little couch in there too, so we should all fit comfortably." He stuck out his hand to Wil. "Thanks for coming up again Wil. This has been amazing, and I hope you know we really appreciate it."

"Of course. When I saw some of the content from the books I had, I knew I wanted to help get them all transcribed or translated or scanned or what have you. I think we have found some important stuff."

The four of them made their way to the office, when he passed his mate, he leaned down to give her a little kiss. "Can you bring us some coffee?"

Jesse was more than a little surprised at the answer. "Nope. I'm on KP. You'll have to make it yourself." He held his breath, waiting for the answer and yelling.

"Well, I guess my cranky ass will make it myself then. Am I on the rotation for KP?" He wasn't angry or upset. Jesse let out the breath he'd been holding.

"You bet you are. I did put you in a little less frequently because of your other duties, but you're on it. I'll make sure you know when it's your day. I know how absent minded you can be." She smiled up at Bryce and Jesse realized they had what Joey would call a healthy relationship.

They made it over to the office and everyone got comfortable. He sat down on a comfy but worn looking couch. Before Rena sat down she looked around at the others. "I made sure there was a fancy little coffee maker with the cups in Jesse's office. Who wants one? While you're trying to get Mariam over here, I will grab some for us." All three men raised their hands. Rena just laughed. "Be right back. I'll bring the cream and stuff over."

Rena left and next to him Wil sighed. "Don't take that for granted. The minute you do it causes problems. Always say thank you. And mean it."

Jesse nodded. "I know. I am so lucky to have found my mates. My mom didn't find hers until just this month. Mom and Dad were best friends and chose to mate and have me. Dad died before finding his. I will always remember to be grateful. And if I forget I have no doubt Rena and Argie and even Mickey will remind me."

~

When Rena returned, they had just managed to get Mariam on the phone and were in the process of saying hello. Apparently, she had headed into town with the pups and her mates to have a family dinner at the diner. They were able to catch her on her cell while her mates were taking the pups for a walk around the town.

"What have you learned that has you so excited?" Mariam's voice came across the speaker phone.

Jesse spoke up, his voice more giddy than usual. "We found a couple of older texts that were basically oral histories that someone decided to write down. This all happened over a hundred years ago. Anyhow, there were many elder members of the kettle at the time that mention legends of a Great War. The reason this is so exciting is because back at the Elders library there was a book that also mentioned it. I just skimmed it a little but haven't actually read that one yet. I will as soon as I get back to Oregon. Anyways, they talk about the Great War between ALL shifters and the fae folk. I think we were all aligned together to fight this war. There is another chapter that talks about a spell that was cast on the shifters."

Mariam's voice filled the room. "Well, from Sam we knew that this was something that had happened. That's one reason he's so determined to fix all these problems, cure this curse or disease or spell, whatever."

"No," Jesse jumped in. "...another spell. A spell that pulled sigmas from all the shifter groups into some sort of, well they call it 'guard' and I'm not sure if it's something that's still happening, but the story said that the guard would wander this world alone but bound in their mission. We still need to figure out a couple of things. Firstly, what exactly a sigma is and secondly, what that mission was. I guess there's a thirdly too, is this still happening?"

Mariam sighed and took her time to answer. "Alright. Make anything about sigmas and any other types of unknown wolves your priority, and anything to do with shifter alliances and also, I want to know if this guard, or whatever it's called, might still exist somehow. And what is their purpose?"

They talked for a few more minutes, decided that they should leave the car there and have Daniel fly them back next week and then they could drive out an SUV with the things that Daniel wanted brought to the campground. When they were done making the plans for the following week and setting a specific schedule of the things that Jesse and Wil should be focusing on with the texts, they ended the call.

"Well," Started Bryce. "I think that went very well. I'm excited to see what y'all are going to find out. I know that the histories are important, but I never realized how beneficial it would be to have someone going over all of them. Each of our families here have bibles. It isn't much but when you're done with the other texts maybe you could enter all of that information into the database you're building as well."

"That sounds great. I will continue to work as quickly but thoroughly as possible. Thanks for setting up this call with Mariam. I really appreciate all of you taking my work seriously. I haven't had a lot of positive feedback with this stuff in the past so I'm grateful." Jesse blushed a bit as he spoke.

Bryce reached over and patted Jesse on the shoulder lightly. "If Mariam didn't understand the importance of all this, and the Elders for that matter, then they wouldn't have asked you. This is a very important job. Especially now when we are seeing that maybe we have forgotten a lot of important stuff. Things that will make a big difference in the shifter world."

Jesse smiled at the man. "Thank you."

*K*yle sat with his mates eating dinner, close enough to Jesse and Bryce to hear how excited they were about something, but not close enough to hear exactly what it was. He liked seeing the joy on Jesse's face though. The young man seemed to already have had so much pain in his life, it was nice to see that he could still find something to smile about.

"This is good, but I need coffee when we're done. Oh, I just remembered that I bought those Jaffa cakes. YES!" Gemma's joy filled voice had both Kyle and Daniel smiling.

"I'm done. Let's clean up and head home. Make a pot of that hazelnut coffee we all like and bust out the cakes." Daniel smiled while he spoke, he seemed as excited to head back to their place as Gemma was. He was looking forward to it too but found himself again worrying about why they were excited. He knew they had both reassured him and he truly believed them, he also doubted because of his past experiences. He didn't want to doubt his mates.

Had no reason to. They had been honest and true with him, and he needed to remember that. It wasn't fair to any of them if he couldn't let go of his insecurities.

The trio cleaned up their plates, putting them in the bins and waved to people as they made their way out. The walk to the clinic was short, it was the building closest to the lodge. Which was nice but also noisy. People were still enjoying dinner and each other's company. Kyle smiled when he saw a few children playing in the clearing between the two buildings. If he wasn't mistaken, they were playing Sardines. He remembered nights as a kid, running around the pack house with all the other kids, playing Sardines, or freeze tag, or hide and seek. He may not have had the best pack in the world, but he had a lot of good memories of growing up. More good than bad. It was more than a lot of people could say.

"I want to help Mariam." He was almost as surprised by his statement as Daniel and Gemma.

Gemma recovered first from the shock. "I get that. She's an amazing Alpha that has a natural way about her that makes her pack want to be better for her, be as giving and caring as her. Her ability to make you want to help others and continue her work is a gift she doesn't even realize she has. She's charismatic and brokers trust like no one else I've ever met."

Daniel nodded in agreement. "The day I met her, she stepped in front of one of those infected wolf beast things to save one of my sisters. She had only known them for about a day. The minute she meets a person she decides to keep them safe. She could've died saving Argie. My sister is alive, so are the twins inside of her, because of Mariam. They weren't even technically in her pack at the time. Just a young girl that needed to be saved, and that's what she did. Then I found out about all the people she helps. Even after I found out about her being The Baker, I didn't fear her. The only people that should ever be afraid of her are the bad people that do bad things."

Kyle stopped dead in his tracks. "Alpha Mariam is The Baker?"

Gemma and Daniel looked at each other and then over to Kyle. Gemma answered. "Yes, but I don't think it's supposed to be public knowledge, we just are in the know because of things that have happened in our own lives."

"I had a great aunt that met her. Helped her. Years ago. She was serving food and drinks at a wedding and apparently it was The Baker's first job. As both the baker and The Baker, if that makes sense. My aunt helped her clean up and make it all go away. She always said that the woman she met was so very young and willing to do anything for the sister she had with her. My aunt is the one that started recommending her to anyone who asked about cakes or catering."

"What happened to your aunt?" Daniel asked

Kyle shrugged. "She passed away about a year later. She wasn't in a healthy relationship. Her parents had married her off when she was young. Her husband was an abusive ass that beat her all the time. That's why she didn't take us when our parents died. She didn't want to invite us into that environment. One day he hit her too hard and that was that." They entered the clinic, closing the door behind them. "The Baker came the next week. At least that was the guess by her pack mates. He was found with his throat slit. Sitting in his recliner, football on the TV and beer cans all around him. Just Desserts magnets found all over the kitchen appliances. I remember thinking that The Baker must've been so mad to do that."

Gemma and Kyle sat at the little breakfast bar while Daniel started their coffee. He finished prepping the press and turned to look at them, leaning his hip against the counter. "Maybe, but more than that, she was smart. She probably wasn't so known yet and in order to get her name out there she needed to start with a bang. Now she doesn't need to advertise or make a statement, it's already done." They were all quiet a moment before Daniel broke the silence again. "How exactly are you hoping to help Mariam?"

Kyle sighed. "I'm not sure. I was thinking mostly about wanting to contribute some way to keeping the people that call her safe. Like Jesse. He called and she made him feel safe, saved him and his mom even. I want to be part of that."

Daniel nodded. "That's a good cause. I've offered her the use of my piloting skills. The pack covers the fuel costs. You should call her tomorrow and let her know you want to help. She'll find a place for you."

"Good. I'd like that. Until then I will just do what I know here. I need to build us a green house and get some crops happening. We need to be way more self-sustaining than we currently are."

Gemma reached down, putting her hand over Kyle's. "I didn't know you liked that kind of gardening or such."

Kyle chuckled. "I have a BS in agriculture with a focus in sustainable solutions. I'm just an old hippie hiding in a young guy's body."

Daniel and Gemma both laughed. Daniel poured them each a cup of coffee and grabbed the fancy creamer from the fridge, passing it to his mates and then grabbing the half and half for himself. They all fixed up their mugs to their liking and, grabbing the Jaffa cakes, they made their way upstairs.

Gemma led them to the small couch and sat down. "One of you pick a movie to watch. I want to veg and cuddle for a little while."

Kyle let Daniel pick the movie since he didn't really care what they watched. Gemma's only request was that it be anything but a romance movie. They settled on a Sci-Fi action movie with sexy leading characters and got comfy on the couch.

It didn't take too long for the snacks and coffee to disappear. Kyle set all of their mugs on the little table next to the couch.

They continued to watch the movie and from his peripheral vision he could see Daniel occasionally adjusting himself. Daniel had his arm over the back of the couch and his hand resting on Gemma's shoulder. Kyle was holding Gemma's hand.

Kyle gave a little sigh and leaned his head onto Gemma. He loved this. Sitting and cuddling with his mates.

Daniel's hand that had been resting on Gemma's shoulder started rubbing the back of Kyle's neck. It felt wonderful. He snuck a glance to see Daniel's face, wondering what he was thinking. All he saw was Daniel smiling down at him. Kyle didn't feel pressure or expectations from what he saw. Just a smile, simple and real.

Gemma pulled up the hand that she was holding and rubbed it along her cheek before kissing the back of his hand. She turned her face to him and smiled. "Can I kiss you?" He nodded his head. "Give me the words mate."

Daniel had to swallow before he could speak. "Please kiss me."

She didn't have to be told twice. She shifted her body, turning a little and leaned in towards him. The kiss was soft and slow, no rushing urgency like they had felt before. Daniel was feeling more like himself now. She tasted of coffee and sugar, and he loved it. He opened his eyes when he felt the couch move. Daniel scooted in tighter behind Gemma and bent his head to start kissing her neck. He wanted those lips on him too.

They kissed and touched for a little longer until finally Gemma moaned and pulled back. "Take me to bed mates. I want to lay with you and make love to you."

They moved quickly to the bedroom and undressed before climbing into their bed. Daniel sighed. "I can't wait until my king bed gets here; we are too many people for this small bed."

Gemma and Daniel both chuckled at his annoyed tone.

They all moved onto the bed, putting Kyle in the middle. He didn't want to complain, but he hoped they wouldn't be disappointed when he wasn't up for more than some making out. He knew they had said they understood that, but he still had a bit of fear that they didn't really mean it.

"Are you alright? Your scent just changed, a lot." Daniel asked the question quietly while putting his arm around Kyle.

"I was just thinking, I know you both have told me multiple times now, but…"

The kiss was quick and light. He looked up into

Gemma's eyes. She was smiling and looked exasperated at the same time. "Stop it."

He smiled back. It was impossible to not smile at Gemma. "Sorry."

"We were perfectly fine kissing and cuddling on the couch. What did we do that changed your mood?" Daniel's question was more than fair. He just hated that he had to answer and even now he knew he was being ridiculous. He opened his mouth to answer but before he could, Gemma spoke up.

"Is this because we put you in the middle? You feel like we are expecting something?"

He shrugged, he didn't want to admit she was right, but he wouldn't lie to her either. "I still am uncertain. I know I shouldn't be and I'm trying to remember all the things you've told me and that I truly believe you, but sometimes it's hard."

Gemma gave him another soft kiss while Daniel hugged him tight and pulled him closer with his arm. Daniel leaned in and shared his kisses with Gemma and Kyle both. "I know that it won't happen overnight. Just let us know if it doesn't stop feeling that way after a few months or so. I would think that would be enough time to gain some faith in us. But if that doesn't happen then either Gemma and I need to figure out what we are doing wrong or we at least need to sit down and really talk out how to overcome this. Because it hurts us when we feel the mistrust and confusion coming from you. Our bond is developing so fast, so strong, and I think that will help you too." He leaned in and kissed Kyle again. This time it didn't stay sweet and soft. It was hard and needy and filled with emotion. "Kiss us, hold us, that's all we're asking for. If you don't feel up for that then just let us know."

Kyle sighed. "I always want to hold you two. Kiss you and taste the desire in the air. I love it."

Kyle looked up to see Gemma smile and lean over him to reach Daniel and share some sweet kisses with him. Kyle felt like an idiot for breaking the mood and he didn't want to feel that way. He took a deep breath and closed his eyes. When he opened them again both of his mates were looking at him.

"Better?" Gemma stroked her fingers down his cheek while she asked.

He nodded before reaching up and pulling Gemma down for more kisses.

The three of them cuddled and kissed for what seemed like ages. Gemma had somehow ended up on top of Kyle, straddling his hips, while Daniel was slowly kissing his way down her back and hips.

Gemma rolled her hips into Kyle and seemed to notice for the first time that he was hard. She paused for a moment and looked at Kyle. He knew she was probably confused by his body's reactions. He gave a nod and she smiled, continuing her rolling movements while he took her mouth in another searing kiss.

Gemma threw her head back and moaned. Kyle wasn't sure why but assumed it was because of whatever Daniel was doing. He rubbed his hand down her back until he felt Daniel's hand rubbing her ass and hip. He brought her face back towards him. "What is Daniel doing that has you so excited?"

When she didn't answer at first, he thought that maybe he'd gone too far. Pushed his newfound dominance onto the wrong mate, but then he saw her blush and look into his eyes.

"He's licking me. Touching me." She moaned again. "He just put another finger in me. It feels so good. He's licking and sucking all over me." She couldn't help but to turn her head and look down her body at Daniel. "Your tongue feels so good inside of me."

She turned back around and soon Gemma was kissing Kyle again. She was getting so wet that Kyle could feel her all over him. Kyle could see she was still needy and wanting more.

"Make love to our mate Daniel. She needs you."

Daniel wasted no time in getting himself lined up behind Gemma and surging into her. The feeling of satisfaction and contentment that came across their bond almost had Kyle coming. Daniel started moving in a slow and calculating rhythm. Gemma was rocking her hips back onto him and making small needy noises.

"More Daniel. Faster. Let her feel how amazing we both think she is. Let her feel how much we want her."

There was no more talking. Gemma alternated between kissing Kyle and arching her back in an attempt to crest that peak.

"No more teasing Daniel, give her what she needs." Daniel nodded at the instruction. Every time Kyle gave him an order it released a little more stress in his body.

Daniel leaned down, holding Gemma tightly between them, and rested his head on Kyle's.

"Kiss me. Please." The words were so sweet Kyle could practically taste them.

"Always." Kyle raised his head that last little bit to bring their lips together. They kissed deep and long and all through it Daniel never slowed down. Pounding himself into their mate. The longer it took the more small and desperate sounds escaped Kyle's mouth. Finally, he pulled back, looking directly into Kyle's eyes.

"Please. Help her, I can't hold on much longer." He accentuated his words with a sudden deep thrust that had all of them gasping.

Kyle reached his hand down and felt where his mates were joined. The soft, wet sounds that they made were like a favorite song. The feeling of Daniel's hard length filling Gemma over and over was beautiful. He kept touching them and stroking them, even while they still moved. His hand was wet from their lovemaking. He used those wet fingers to play with Gemma, roll her clit between his fingers and when she seemed to want more, he gave it to her. A pinch, a squeeze, a rolling caress. He loved how every time he touched her, she gasped and rolled her hips again. Finally, he moved his hand to her ass and started rubbing those wet fingers on her tight hole. He didn't try to penetrate her or force her into it, just teased lightly until she was begging for release too.

Poor Daniel was waiting on her and Kyle could see the strain.

"What do you need love?" Gemma shook her head like she didn't know, then opened her eyes and looked down at Kyle.

"I need his bite too."

Daniel heard her plea and immediately dropped his mouth to her shoulder and bit down. Hard. Right next to the marks that had been left by Kyle just the day before.

Gemma screamed and shook while the orgasm rushed through her. Daniel was right behind her.

They all collapsed into a heap of sweaty limbs.

Kyle was running his hands up and down his mates' backs.

Daniel finally caught his breath and looked into Kyle's eyes. "You don't need?"

"I have everything I need. I feel like myself again, happy to cuddle, satisfied by simply that. And bossing you around a little. Go to sleep, you were such a good boy." He leaned over, giving Daniel a light kiss before getting comfortable and closing his eyes.

It had been a productive evening. Jesse was happy with how much he and Wil had gotten done. He was happy to be back at their cabin though. Too many people in such a short period of time. It was hard on him. He knew he had to deal with it eventually and he was hoping that all the therapy would eventually help. He looked over towards the kitchen where his beautiful mate was getting a couple of sodas out of the fridge. Even if he never got any better, he was just starting to understand that they would all love him anyways. He didn't know what he'd done to deserve so much.

"Let's do this puzzle for a while. I haven't done a puzzle in forever and I actually find it really relaxing." Rena spoke while she was busy digging out said puzzle and clearing off the table.

"Sounds nice. Mom and I used to do puzzles all the time too. Want me to make some popcorn?" He asked while making his way to their small kitchen.

Rena scrunched her nose in the special way that made

him smile and meant she was thinking. "No, let's do the pretzels instead. I don't want to get the puzzle all buttery and I don't want to eat popcorn that isn't disgustingly covered with butter."

Jesse laughed. "Got it." He quickly grabbed a bowl and poured some of the pretzels into it and got comfortable at the table next to his mate. "This puzzle is going to take forever, it's almost all the same color!"

Rena laughed a little maniacally. "Just be glad I'm not insisting that we do it upside down like my sister does. She says it evens the playing field."

"Nope. I'm not looking forward to that."

They sat comfortably and made some good progress while eating their pretzels and just talking about nothing and everything.

They'd been at it for a good period of time and had grown quiet. In fact, it was so quiet in the room that Jesse could hear the carbonation in their sodas against the sides of the aluminum cans. He took a moment to look at Rena and think about how he was going to say what he wanted to say. He always ended up tongue tied, and he didn't want that.

"Thank you for being patient with me. I know that I come with a lot of baggage, and I might not be the ideal you dreamt of when you were younger, but you always make me feel good. You make it easy to be your mate. I want you to know how much I appreciate that."

She looked at him with that little scrunched nose and then sighed. "You are… you. I am aware how lucky I am to have found my mate so young. I know Argie feels the same way about Chris and Mickey. We've talked about how lucky we are. We all have issues. Everyone in the world has issues. I figure you and Mickey and Chris are better off than Argie and me when it comes to issues. We still have to figure out what our issues are." She smiled and just that simple smile made him feel better. "Honestly though, all joking aside, I am so grateful to have found you." She reached out her hand and put it on top of Jesse's.

He was cold. He knew the weather was going to keep getting colder and the smart move would be heading south, but for some reason he felt the need to head west. He didn't realize how many different pack lands he was going to have to cross, and between that and being hunted by whoever was following him, it was making sleep or even stopping to rest a problem. He was in animal form currently, holding his meager belongings in his mouth, and trying his best to find some sort of shelter before the sun set. He heard a train in the distance, too far to catch tonight, but tomorrow he'd head that direction and try to hop on, like a hobo in the old days. As long as the train was going the right direction. He finally found a small hollow under a tree. It wasn't great but if he stayed in shifted form, it should be enough. He stowed his small bag and started looking for some food. He'd been eating in this form for a few weeks now. He was craving fried chicken but the bunny he was scenting would have to do. He finally caught the poor creature and put it out of its misery as fast as possible. He hated this. He looked up at a friendly looking sign for a cafe in Grand Forks. He hadn't realized he'd gotten close enough to the road to see

billboards. He quickly finished his meal and made his way back to his belongings and the little spot he'd sleep tonight. It really was getting colder earlier. What did he expect in September this far north? He made himself comfortable and huddled down, curling around himself to get as small as possible and with his tail over his nose. He didn't know why he wasn't going as far south as possible. He should be heading for Florida or Southern California, but his animal said west was the way to go. He'd just started to doze off when he heard a twig snap...

Jesse opened his eyes and saw the concerned face of his mate looking down at him. They were still alone in their cabin, but he was on the bed. "Did you carry me to the bed?"

Rena smirked at him. "It's not like I'm a strong wolf or anything."

Jesse smiled. "Can you hand me my journal?" He sat up and stretched his neck and shoulders. "How long was I out?"

"About an hour. If you hadn't woken in the next few minutes I would've gone for Gemma." She handed him the journal and a pencil.

"I saw our mate again. It was September. But who knows if that means this year or what?" Jesse carefully wrote out his vision while talking. "Also, I think our mate is a jaguar. Which is making me laugh because he's coming from the east and I would think jaguars would naturally be from the south." He smiled but it quickly faded. "I hope we can find him. This is the second vision

I've had of him being hunted. Hey, do you think maybe those same wack jobs that attacked the picnic might be the ones hunting him?"

"Who knows. Either way we need to find him before whoever is hunting him does."

"I've been thinking about the attack. Or actually, to be more specific, the group of shifters that attacked us."

Kyle's voice broke the silence. They'd all been awake for a while but simply enjoying staying in bed for as long as they could get away with.

"What were you thinking?" Gemma looked over her shoulder at Kyle.

"Well, it seems odd to me that so many different types of shifters would be working together. Not just that either, they were working together to kill a large number of shifters. I'm thinking it's weird that so many of us didn't even know about other types of shifters until recently, and according to Beppie the hawks weren't aware of other shifters either, so how did these guys, A- find each other and, B- know about all these other shifters they want to kill. And why do they want to attack us? The entire situation is strange."

That thought hung in the air while they seemed to all

be mulling it over. Eventually Daniel was the one that broke the silence. "Jesse found something that indicated that we knew about each other in the past. Maybe these guys just never forgot. Perhaps they were a collective or commune or who knows what in some isolated location. Just saying that out loud sounds ridiculous. Maybe Jesse will find more information in the books that will help. I know he's been excited about finding out a lot more. I really hope he does because you're right, we have no information on these guys or what's driving them."

Kyle slid out of bed and stretched. "I think we need to see if Jesse needs or more accurately wants help. I have a feeling he doesn't need much help with the books but if we have a deadline or the urgency of this current situation, he might allow us to assist him."

"I can't today, I promised the kettle that I'd have an open clinic day for anyone that needs a regular checkup. The basics, so I'm not expecting any emergencies, just a very long day. I'm going to make it a weekly thing until everyone in town has a chance to be seen. For everything else I'm doing appointments only, except of course the emergencies."

Kyle looked at Daniel with a hopeful face. Daniel sighed but smiled. "Fine. I will also help. But I thought you were going to talk to Bryce today about starting some green houses and such."

"I am, but I won't be able to start on the actual building part yet. I need to do a bit of other stuff first. Today I just need to get permission for my ideas. So, I'm going to take a quick shower and then I'll make us all some coffee and maybe even eggs." He smiled at both of his mates before turning and heading into the restroom.

Kyle was fast but not fast enough apparently. He stepped out to an empty bedroom and sounds in the kitchen downstairs. He smiled to himself and threw on some sweats before heading down.

Gemma was sitting at the bar with a hot cup of coffee in her hands, watching Daniel make something. They were laughing at something one of them had said. They looked so happy. The last step was creaky, and they both turned to look at him, their eyes glowed with joy and happiness, and it made his breath catch in his throat for a moment. Gemma cocked her head to the side and smiled. "You doing ok?"

Kyle nodded and let out the breath that had been stuck in his chest. "I'm great. I'm just not used to having mates yet, not used to seeing anyone looking at me like… like you do. I didn't know it would feel like this."

Daniel split the eggs he'd been cooking on three plates before turning around and smiling up at Kyle. "I was thinking the same thing when I woke up this morning. Like a punch to the gut and I couldn't catch my breath. The idea that I have finally found the people I will be with forever, the people that will be mine until the day I die, in the very distant future I might add. So yeah, I know what you mean."

Kyle smiled and made his way over to Kyle, reaching out to pull the man into a tight hug. "You two are more than I ever could've hoped for."

They stood there just holding each other for a minute or two before Gemma spoke up. "Hey, my eggs are getting cold. And I want some hugs too."

～

hen they finished breakfast, and a little cuddling, Daniel and Kyle walked over to Jesse's office, leaving Gemma home to get ready for her patients. The door to the office was open but Daniel knocked on the door frame anyhow. Jesse looked up to greet them with sleepy eyes. Kyle wondered why he didn't sleep well. There could have been any number of fun reasons to stay up late, innocent and otherwise, but the look in his eyes made Kyle think it hadn't been a fun time. The young man smiled and tried his best anyhow.

"Hey guys, what's up?"

It was Daniel that took the lead, as Kyle preferred. In public anyhow. He felt himself smile at that and realized he'd missed the beginning of Daniel speaking. "...if you've seen anything about that."

Jesse seemed to think it over before replying. "No. Nothing about a falling out or incident between shifters. The opposite actually. In the few very old texts I've seen, and I'm talking a thousand years old, texts that would have long disintegrated if it wasn't for some sort of magics placed on them... what was I saying? Oh, yeah, the older books and scrolls talk about shifter groups working together. I scanned one this morning, talking about how the pack frequently let geese shifters, which I'd never heard of, and cougar shifters stay with them when they traveled through the area. The guests would usually help hunt and tell the pack news from other packs; it was the only way information was passed. Wil was telling me that he saw a family bible where almost every generation for as far back as it went had at least one person marrying into a bear clan. That all stopped a long time ago. And it stopped abruptly which is peculiar. It might give us a rough timeline of when things started changing though."

They passed theories back and forth for a while and must've lost track of time because soon Rena was walking in with a couple of sodas and sandwiches in her hands. "Oh hey. Didn't know you'd be here, or I would've grabbed a couple more sandwiches from the line."

Kyle looked out and saw that today's kitchen crew was serving up sandwiches and what looked to be potato salad. "We can leave you to have your lunch."

"That's alright, you can stay if you'd like." Rena was genuine in her comment.

"No, we need to bring Gemma some lunch. She's been working all morning; she won't stop for food unless we make her." Daniel smiled down at his sister. He gave her a quick kiss on the top of her head on his way out.

Both Kyle and Daniel grabbed some food, enough for all of them, and walked back to the clinic. As they were setting down the food on the breakfast bar the exam room opened. "Just make sure to finish the antibiotics, don't just stop when you start feeling better. We're shifters, not invincible." She handed over a bottle of medicine to the older man and shook his hand. He gave her a nod of his head and left.

"We brought food."

Jesse smiled at Rena while she set everything down and pulled up a chair to the other side of the desk. When she noticed him staring and smiling she smiled back. "What? You were busy. I figured if I didn't bring you something to eat that you'd end up forgetting all together."

Jesse shrugged. "Probably." He stretched his neck, first one direction then the other. "Thank you for watching out for me."

The two ate their lunch and talked about what they've been doing all day. Jesse threw away the napkins and pulled out his sketch pad. While they kept talking, he doodled. He was busy sketching out the sign from the latest vision when Josh walked in.

"Hey guys, sorry to interrupt. I just wanted to double check something on the computer really quick. I was setting up the Alpha mate's computer in her office and realized I needed to network things differently. I just need to get back there for a sec."

Jesse stood up and moved around to sit in the empty chair next to Rena while Josh took his place. The three made small talk while Josh worked. Suddenly Josh stopped talking mid-sentence. "What's this?" He pointed to the drawing that was sitting on the desk.

"Oh, well, I have visions. That's our third from the latest one I had. We are hoping to figure out where he is so we can find him before he's hurt. We know he's being hunted." Jesse said it matter of factly and wondered how he was able to get the words out without getting choked up.

Josh seemed to be thinking of what to say. Finally, he broke the silence. "I know exactly where that is. I used to head that way for work and have hunted in both forms in that area. It's not too far from here actually."

Rena jumped up, grabbing a pen and paper. "Tell us how to get there. We need to go soon. He's going to be there in the next month or so, we need to be there to help him when he arrives."

Josh smiled at her enthusiasm and wrote down everything he knew about the area. "Promise me you will not try to go save him alone. You two need back up. That area has some not so friendly packs and human hunters alike. It's not a great place to be if you're alone."

Jesse nodded. "I'll let Mariam and Bryce know right now. Promise."

*J*esse finished his work a little early and made his way back to the cabin. He walked in and saw Rena had fallen asleep on the small couch while she read. She looked so beautiful. He didn't want to bother but he really wanted to be close to her at the same time. He tried to sit down quietly next to her without waking her up, unfortunately the movement caused her book to fall to the ground with a loud plop. Rena's eyes shot open.

"Didn't mean to wake you. Just wanted to sit."

Rena smiled at him. "That's fine. I'm feeling … something. I don't know what. I'd like some cuddles if you're up for it."

Jesse smiled back. "I am. I am feeling the need to cuddle too."

He got comfortable on the couch and Rena snuggled under his arm, resting her head on his chest. "Are you nervous? I'm nervous. What if it's not this September and we get our hopes up and then nothing happens. Or, what if we find him. We are just getting used to each other and now we are going to add another person to the mix. What if…"

Jesse leaned down and gave her a quick and almost chaste kiss. "Don't worry. Fate has our back."

"I wanted to tell Mariam about what's going on. My brother said she'll be back tomorrow night. I guess we'll wait until then."

"Did he say where she went?"

Rena sighed. "No, and I asked. He got all shady and stuff and just said that she would be back soon. I think he knows but wherever she went isn't public knowledge."

3 8

$\mathcal{J}$osh checked the message board one more time. He didn't have time for errors. His aunt could only watch his son for the weekend. He didn't have time for mistakes. It wasn't too far. Not this time. He could get over there and back pretty fast, he just hoped he wouldn't have to wait too long when he got there.

He checked his gear a second time and made his way out of town.

❧

$\mathcal{H}$e'd been waiting in the living room for nearly four hours. Finally, he heard the back door. Something wasn't right, whoever was coming in was trying their best to be silent. He silently crept to the back door and waited, back flat against the wall next to the door.

The door opened quietly, then all hell broke loose. He

wasn't sure how the person knew he was there, but they did. They wrestled for what felt like forever but was in actuality was more like ten seconds. He thought he had the upper hand when they finally stopped, his blade held against the other person's neck. That's when he noticed a blade against his thigh, just a small cut there would bleed him out.

"Well," the voice was familiar. "This is interesting."

Mariam quickly backed up a couple of steps. "Why are you here?"

Josh sighed. "I'm guessing we are here for the same reason. And now I'm connecting some dots." He slid his knife back into the leather sheath on his waist. "Hello Baker, I'm The Talon. And this asshole has two people here to kill him."

They probably would've talked more but the asshole in question chose that time to come walking in the door. He looked like he was about to scream. Before he even pulled in the breath to make a sound the man had his jugular and femoral slit. A moment of gurgles and then nothing.

Josh pulled out a rag and cleaned his knife before putting it away. He looked up to see Mariam doing the same. She smiled.

"Well, this is interesting. Tell me more about your night job." Mariam paused and looked around. "Let's go to that waffle place that was around the corner and talk. Killing rapists always makes me hungry."

He nodded his head and laughed. "Me too."

ea watched from where she sat on the bed, changing a tiny diaper, as Tabitha held their son in her arms. She sat in a rocking chair using her feet to set it into motion, humming a little tune under her breath. She would've argued if Bea had said it out loud, but she looked beautiful sitting there in yoga pants and a faded black V-neck, her bare toes painted purple and her hair in a yoga bun.

"What are you looking at?" Tabitha smiled when she asked.

Bea was so lucky to have found her mate at such a young age. So lucky to get to spend decades with this woman that made her smile every day. "I'm just happy."

Tabitha shifted her weight a little. "He is so adorable when he's asleep. Well, all the time really, but especially like this."

"I agree." Bea picked up the pup when she was done with the diaper and carefully put her in the crib next to her sister. "They all are. I can't believe they're actually here. I'm a mom. We're parents. Oh my gosh, we're parents." She looked over at Tabitha who had started laughing at her.

"Don't look so horrified. You are a mom. We have pups. And you are going to be amazing."

They held each other for a couple of minutes before laying down and trying to get a little sleep themselves.

Something woke Bea a couple of hours later. She got up and headed for the crib, assuming the thing that woke her was one of the pups wanting to eat. She saw all three cuddled together, but something wasn't right. She snapped on the little lamp next to the crib and screamed.

"What's wrong?" Tabitha was next to her between one second and the next.

The problem was evident. Their son was convulsing. His color was wrong, like he wasn't getting enough air. Bea reached down and grabbed him. She knew Tabitha would look after the other two. She took off running for the clinic.

She didn't knock. Just ran in and yelled for Gemma. She was crying and didn't know what to do. His little body still shook and now he was almost purple.

Gemma took the pup from her arms while her brother wrapped his arms around her. "Let go, let Gemma look." His voice was loud through all the noise. Then she realized the noise was her, yelling and crying. She stopped abruptly.

It was about an hour later that Gemma finally came

out of the exam room pushing one of the small clear box looking bassinets. There was a hissing noise that Bea realized was oxygen filling the pup's little box. Tabitha sat next to her on the couch, each of them holding a pup. Bea didn't know what to say or do.

Gemma sat down on the coffee table in front of Bea. "Something is wrong. I don't know what. I need to talk to the pup's father. I think this is something genetic because I'm not seeing anything in his blood and as a shifter, he would be able to fight off anything like a virus in a matter of hours. But honestly, I don't know." Gemma sighed. "Can you get him here? I need blood samples and to get a full medical family history."

Bea and Tabitha looked at each other for a minute before Bea got up, handing the pup she was holding over to Daniel. She made her way over to the phone and dialed.

"Hello?" The voice was sleepy but sounded like the right one... maybe?

"Neville? It's me Bea."

There was silence. "This isn't Neville. This is Chuck. His brother."

"Oh, sorry, you sound similar. Is Neville there? I know it's late but it's important."

"Neville is dead. Car accident two weeks ago. I've been going through his things and paperwork and your name popped up. What did you do to get him to leave everything to you and someone named Tabitha? Are you some kind of con woman? Because I will fight you. I am meeting with the lawyer tomorrow. You aren't getting a penny."

Bea was frozen. "No, he can't be dead. I need him. Something is wrong with the pup. I need samples and family history; the doctor needs it. The pup can't breathe. I don't…. Let me talk to Neville."

The pause on the other end of the line seemed to go on forever. "What pup?"

"My pup. Neville gave us pups, and something is wrong."

Bea started crying again and couldn't stop. Kyle came over and took the phone from her. "Hey, I'm Kyle, Bea's brother. Neville was the donor for my sister and her mate. My sister had the pups, but one is really, really sick." He seemed to be listening for a bit before he continued. "Sure. We are at the campground outside of Hawk's Landing." He gave directions to the campground before saying thank you and hanging up.

"He will be here in two days." He looked to Gemma "The father is dead. But his brother will be here. They were triplets. Apparently, this guy Chuck is the last one. Neville and the other triplet were together in the car when it went off the cliff. I hope his DNA works to answer the questions you have. I hope it's enough to save my nephew."

ACKNOWLEDGMENTS

A big thank you to my kids. They let me hide in my room and write. Thank you to Kelly and Jami for making me be accountable to my own deadlines. I appreciate you all. You make it so much easier to be what I've wanted to be for decades.

Thank you.

ABOUT THE AUTHOR

Maggie Decker is a widowed mother of four and Giagia to a couple of feral cuties. Her first book *Just Desserts* was released in 2016 and it changed her life. Maggie is a big nerd that loves trivia games and watching comic book shows. She can often be found holding a cup of coffee and procrastinating.

amazon.com/Maggie-Decker/e/B084WQX7WY?
ref=sr_ntt_srch_lnk_1&qid=1648621217&sr=8-1

Hidden Pack

Just Desserts

Adam took this job to stay out of trouble. He was happy with his life and didn't want to start anything that would change it. Staying out of trouble was a great plan, right up to the moment he saw her.

Mariam can do it on her own. Her wolf abandoned her long ago and she learned to live without her. She has spent years making sure she belongs to no known pack and never will.

Ben has loved his life with Adam, but he has to wonder, is there still a place for him in Adam's new life?

Things haven't been right for a while now. Attacks have been happening between normally friendly people, and that is just one oddity. On top of that there is a crazed mutant that seems to have a desire to kill and memories are haunting more than one person of a similar crime.

Can Mariam make sense of it all? But more importantly can she learn to take help from the people around her. Will she realize she's no longer alone? Can these three survive being thrown together for life?

When things start unraveling and people start getting hurt can they come together to help save the innocent or are hurt feelings going to win?

Worth The Wait

Elkan's had over 25 years to be angry about being abandoned by his mate. How long will forgiveness take?

Joey ran away with nothing more but the memories of what could've been. He needed to protect his sister, and he'd do it again. That doesn't mean it was easy.

Now, by chance, they find each other again and have to decide if they can make it work this second time around. They need to figure it out pretty quickly too, because like always, life continues on and their help is needed.

People are being attacked and if they work together, with the help of their pack and their family, they just might be able to save lives.

In the end they might discover that this is how fate always meant it to be and that even through all the pain, it was worth the wait.

Creature's Comfort

Tom has been rejected from the only pack he had. His body and soul broken until only anger was left. Can he find the strength to trust again?

Sam has been looking for his mate for nearly a century. When he finally meets him he's greeted with only disdain and hostility. Is there any way to earn the trust of someone who hates you without reason?

He has no name. None that he can remember. His tormented soul is trapped inside a body that has become a prison. Only vague memories of who he once was remind him he was ever more than this. Without hope he is ready to let go, but at the moment of capture he senses a second chance to get back what once was lost.

Can these three work together to save each other before what could be becomes what never was?

The beast they captured opens the door to the answers Alpha has been looking for and opens the eyes of the Hidden Pack to another world they never knew existed.

And Mariam's story that started it all

The Baker

Before she was Alpha of Hidden Pack she was simply a child.

Mariam watched, helpless, as her life became something she hated. A life of uncertainty and fear.

With her parents gone her brother changed into someone she didn't even recognize

and could no longer trust...or even love.

When the unthinkable happens she runs as far and as fast as she can. She never hoped for more than a safe space to lay her head.

When the chance at a new life presents itself she can't say no.

A new life.

A new home.

A new family.

...And she will do anything to protect them.

Ghost and the Hanged Man

Ghost

I was an outcast. alone . Spending life in the shadows, watching; unwilling to claim what little family I have. I've lived on the outskirts of Ruby Gulch my entire life, learning early how to take care of myself when I didn't want anyone else to do it. Magic flows beneath me, through me, and one day that magic brings me a man.

Penny

I never regretted taking care of my family, or wished for an easier life; not until the day my family needed something I couldn't provide. I made my way to Ruby Gulch in search of the man who owed us a debt. Instead of offering me help he offered me a rope. There was a feeling of magic in Ruby Gulch and somehow that magic saved me. Can I save my family?

When the two men meet they decide to try again, to look for the help they want. What they find is something different all together, not the help they were looking for but maybe it was what they needed. Now the magic is in danger and only they can save Ruby Gulch and the power beneath it.

www.ingramcontent.com/pod-product-compliance
Lightning Source LLC
Chambersburg PA
CBHW020318160726
47992CB00004B/1601